Flight to Spain

One Man's Andalusian Odyssey

Kenneth Fretwell

1

My name is Ken Fretwell and at fifty I have achieved the goal that I set for myself almost a year earlier, although now that I've achieved it I'd better set myself another goal soon to keep me on my toes. I've set and achieved goals for myself several times before, however, so I'm getting used to that feeling of restlessness by now and I suppose it happens to everybody. This is the first time that I've set pen to paper in earnest for over fifteen years and I guess that the fact that I feel I've done something arguably worth writing about should be some consolation.

For the fifteen years before I went to Spain – note the coincidence in dates – I worked as an employment adviser, which entailed helping people who wanted to find a job to find one and people who didn't want to find a job to want one. Friends who knew I'd once done a little writing said that my job must be terribly interesting, that I must meet some real characters, and that I really ought to write about it. Everybody thinks everybody else's job must be interesting, of course, but apart from the wicked glee I felt every time I tricked somebody who didn't want a job into getting one, for the most part it was like watching badly-dressed, under or over-nourished and sometimes abusive paint dry. (I told you I hadn't written for fifteen years.) I might come back to this subject in the form of pertinent flashbacks, but then again I might not. I'll warn you now that I favour a sort of 'stream of consciousness' approach to writing this story, but I promise not to wander from the subject more than I have to.

Before I transport you out of England, however, a bit of background information is in order, I think, as you'll not want to set foot on Spanish soil with the empty husk of a man, will you? Having said that, after I've told you where I was up to in my life before I made my momentous decision, you'll probably conclude that an empty husk of a man was precisely what I was. Although I don't want to hide too many things from you, neither do I wish to upset or annoy (probably just annoy) my ex-wife and her entourage, so I'll just say that after divorcing at forty-six and settling our financial affairs more or less amicably and fairly, especially for her, and with my son and daughter already in their early twenties, I felt a great sense of liberation. My ex-wife felt this too, she claimed, but it didn't stop her marrying another man only fourteen months after our divorce, suggesting that the merest whiff of liberation, closely followed by the stronger scent of a doctor's salary, had been sufficient for her. No sour grapes though.

Anyway, this liberation business was fun for a while, but it didn't change my tiresome job and it meant that I couldn't afford to buy a house in the small Derbyshire town where I had spent most of my life. (I'll be more precise about places once I'm in Spain, I promise.) People who rented in my town were always looked down upon by people who owned, so rather than feeling like a liberated man I felt like a liberated failure, which is not the same thing at all. I took up cycling again to rejuvenate myself and restore my self-esteem, but found that the roads were much busier, the hills much steeper and the cold much colder than in my youth, so my self-esteem went down rather than up and I took to going out of an evening (to the pub, not on my bike). There I found that the beer was much dearer, the conversations more boring, the televisions everywhere, and the chance of meeting women *infinitely* more difficult than in my youth so, it then being mid-March, I got my old road bike out again and started to pedal in earnest.

I found that the more I pedalled the better I felt, but while my cycling made me feel more satisfied with myself physically, it had the adverse effect of making my job seem more frustrating and tedious than ever. I put this down to the endorphins produced by cycling making me feel good, but not lasting long enough to carry on making me feel good the next day at work. I tried cycling to work – about seven miles – but either that was not far enough, or the fact that half the time I got wet through, meant that it was not the solution. Short of setting up a static bike in an empty office and spending ten minutes of every hour pedalling away on it, I saw that cycling would not cure me of my workplace malaise, so I decided to use my next period of post-cycling exhilaration to do some serious positive and constructive thinking.

One Sunday afternoon, after cycling over 40 miles for the first time without reaching home in a pitifully fatigued state, I showered, ate and decided that the time was ripe to set myself one of my goals. Before I describe that afternoon's events, perhaps I should quickly tell you what my previous accomplished goals have been. The ones I can remember are: passing my A levels, earning my second category road racing (cycling) licence, not failing my degree, getting into teaching, marrying my ex-wife, getting out of teaching, and divorcing my ex-wife. Whether there were any more goals that I didn't achieve, I can't remember, as my memory is as selective as the next man's, but I solemnly set myself and achieved the abovementioned ones, elements of which I may come back to later on if, and only if, they add to my story. If there's one thing I hate it's waffling and as I've just summarised two thirds of my life in less than a paragraph, I'm not doing too badly so far.

So, I took my pen, a large pad and an energy-restoring drink to the kitchen table and resolved not to move until I had set my next major life goal. I wrote JOB in capital letters and circled it. I wrote TOWN in capital letters and circled that, before doing the same with the word MONEY and settling down to scrutinise my equilateral, existential, triangle. I then wrote the word AGE in the middle, before joining up the sides of the triangle and appraising my handiwork. (This may seem a little pedantic, but it's what I actually did, and it worked.)

I first centred my thoughts on the word JOB and within two minutes had decided conclusively and irrefutably that it had to go, or rather that I had to go. I'd got into that line of work in order to get out of teaching, despite the pay cut, and given that I couldn't afford to buy a half decent house anyway, I could just as easily take another pay cut if necessary and get out of my latest rut. I then moved onto TOWN (meaning mine) and concluded that it no longer held any special attraction for me. As far as responsibilities went, my children were away studying, my father had died, and my mother was living with my younger brother and his family in

Brighton, so, apart from a few pals, there wasn't much to hold me there.

So, I pondered, was it to be a new job in a new town? I thought of all the places I had visited in Britain and apart from some out the way areas in the north of England, Wales and Scotland, where I'd be unlikely to find a job or pay the rent if I did, there was nowhere that appealed to me any more than my home town. Feeling a mental impasse coming on, I finished my drink and moved onto MONEY and AGE.

As far as money went I wasn't badly off at all and could live without working for at least a year if I could think of a good reason for not doing so. It would have to be a good reason as I was well aware that I could do this once and once alone, and if I squandered the time I would probably regret it until my dying day. Moving onto AGE I realised that my dying day was now almost certainly nearer than the day I was born – I didn't know of anybody who had lived to 98 in my family – and that if the worst came to the worst the state would support me just like it supported the hundreds of people I had been 'advising' for so many years. Being well-informed about these things, I knew that I only needed to pay in for another three or four years to secure my state pension, which, added to my little teaching pension and another small private one, meant that I only really had the next sixteen years to worry about.

This was indeed food for thought and the idea of spending the next sixteen years doing my frustrating job in my dull town sent a little shiver of mortality down my spine and sent me over to the fridge for a beer. After a restorative sip or two, I put my later life out of my mind and wrote the number 50 on my pad. My next goal, I decided, would be accomplished by the time I was fifty, so all I had to do was decide what the goal was to be.

After a nutritious dinner, for I can cook well enough, I adjourned to the local pub for a drink and my trip there produced the following effects for the following reasons. The reasons which led to the effects were the stultifying conversations I had with my cronies there, all held above, or beneath, the din of yet another televised football match, and the fact that I drank five pints, a lot for me. The effects thus caused were my swearing to myself that I would leave my job and my town before the year was out and that by the time I was fifty *I would be somewhere I liked, doing something that I liked doing.* When I got home I wrote this down on my sheet.

The following morning a dry mouth and slight headache did nothing to diminish my resolve and I put my now quite cluttered sheet of paper into my jacket pocket in order to muse on it between sob stories, lies and the odd assertion from the person in front of me that he or she really *did* want to find a job. By lunchtime I had decided that I must go to live in another country. By 5 o'clock I had decided that the country would be Spain. By bedtime I had decided that I would cycle there.

The next day the receipt of a hefty gas bill in the post did much to strengthen my resolve, but before I go on I ought to explain how I reached my momentous decision, or decisions. I decided on Spain (and we'll soon be there, I promise you) because, as well as the good weather, I have a Spanish A level and I reasoned that it would be the easiest language for me to learn, or relearn. Also, on my five holidays there over the years and despite rarely venturing out of the coastal tourist meccas, I had found the few Spaniards I had conversed with to be friendly souls and I hoped that some of their benign and carefree nature would rub off on me and help to wash away the metaphorical grime of my depressing job and restore the wholly positive outlook on life which I had last enjoyed when I was cycle racing back in the eighties.

This brings us to the foolish idea of cycling there. Before I go on I'd better point out right now that in the end I shelved the idea of actually cycling *to* Spain after concluding that riding to Portsmouth or Plymouth to catch the ferry to Bilbao or Santander would be a tiresome, dangerous and, in all likelihood, wet experience. I then decided that at least 24 hours on the ferry would also be quite onerous as I have always been prone to seasickness. Given, then, that I would be flying there, I saw little point in starting in the north when the area that interested me was the south, mainly due to the climate, so I finally settled on flying to Malaga and setting off from there.

Was it a cop out? Call it that if you wish, but I've never been the heroic type and the main thing was to get myself to Spain and onto my bike, rather than breaking down, mechanically or psychologically, somewhere near Swindon and going home with my morale crushed. Who wants to read about someone riding from Derbyshire to the south coast, anyway? Not that I was thinking of writing about it then, but I have no regrets about taking the easy option as the route I finally took was quite tough enough for me. If you really want to read about cycling heroics, read *Sting in the Tail: by Racing Bicycle around the World*, by Peter Duker, if you can get hold of it, for it is long out of print. It's the worst written, most entertaining book about cycling exploits that I've ever read, but I digress.

Returning to the actual sequence of events, once I had decided that I would fly to Malaga, with bike and all, I then had to decide when I was going to set off and what, if anything, I was going to do once I got there, apart from tour around on the comfortable touring bike that I intended to purchase. One option, of course, would be to just take a six month sabbatical from work and 'find myself' in Spain, only to lose myself again as soon as I got back to my desk. No, setting off *knowing* that I was going to return would be no more than an extended holiday which would give me a taste for a work-free life in a warm country; a taste which would turn bitter on me once I came back, skint and condemned to live in England for ever and ever, or at least until I died.

I did like the word 'sabbatical', though, and I decided to ask for one at work.

"How long do you want?" asked my boss, Graham, precisely the kind of mouldering husk of a man in his late fifties who I did not want to become. Nice chap though.

"Six months, I think. I want to cycle round Spain."

"Can't you do that in a month?"

"I cycle slowly. Besides, I need a break. I'm going stale."

"Your divorce still affecting you, is it?" he asked.

"Not really."

"Yes, it is," he nodded fervently, making his chins wobble.

"Is it?"

"Yes. Sabbaticals aren't really the done thing here, you see. We don't earn enough for a start. You have to be having some sort of crisis, the more traumatic the better."

"I'm having a crisis," I replied sadly.

"Good. When do you want to go?"

"Is the first of September all right?"

"I'll sort it," he said, before lumbering back to his office.

The good thing about asking for a sabbatical was that it provided me with a kind of safety net. The bad thing was that I might get cold feet, even in the warmth of Andalusia, and scurry back to security after the winter was over, so I told myself, repeatedly, to put the lovely word sabbatical out of my mind, as come January or February I would be ringing Graham to tell him that I'd decided to extend my sabbatical indefinitely.

All this gave me a nice warm feeling for a few days, but I knew all too well that my sabbatical (I know, I'm wearing the word out) would come to an end, one way or another, and that I'd better think about how I could actually earn a living in Spain. An evening on the internet taught me that I could teach English, work in the tourist industry on the coast, or sell houses. The internet also taught me, however, that the latter option would hardly be practicable after the bursting of the Spanish housing bubble had left over a million properties unoccupied. I'm no salesman anyway.

Well, I used to be a teacher – of History, which uses English a lot – so I looked into that line of work more closely. It appeared that as well as all my qualifications and experience I would also probably need something called a TEFL certificate (Teaching English as a Foreign Language), that I would have to take a month long, full-time course to get one, and that it would set me back over a thousand pounds. I didn't like the sound of all that time and money as I wasn't all that keen on teaching again anyway, so I concluded that if I took along photocopies of all my certificates and references I *might* just be able to wangle my way into some lesser language school on the strength of my pedagogical past.

So teaching was one option, tourism was another, and surely there were other ways to make a living there, so long as I knew the language. After all, millions of Spaniards have jobs, though a couple of million less than a couple of years ago, and we are all in the same European Union after all. Well, one line of thought led to another and I realised that in order to access about 99% of all Spanish jobs I would have to speak Spanish, which reminded me that I didn't speak it very well at all.

This led in turn to yet more internet research and intense thought, after which I reached the conclusion that the thing to do was to buy a good grammar book, a good exercise book (not a blank one, but one full of exercises) and some DVDs of films with English subtitles. This I did towards the end of May and by August I was completely fluent. Joking aside, I did make very good progress and used my fortnight's holiday in July (which Graham refused to allow me to tag onto my sabbatical, despite my insistence that a nervous breakdown was fast approaching) as a study and cycling 'boot camp' which increased my vocabulary and reduced my weight considerably. I'm five foot eleven and then weighed just over twelve stone, by the way.

During all this time I had also been perusing that famous internet auction site in search of a good, solid touring bike. I could have bought a new one, but, if I'm perfectly honest, I quite liked the idea of looking like a seasoned veteran of many a cycle tour rather than an impulsive twerp, so second hand it had to be. In the first week of August I finally found what I was looking for within the thirty mile radius of my search area. The bike was, and still is, a used but unabused silver Dawes (Galaxy) with a 23 inch aluminium frame, chrome forks, 24 gears, fairly fat tyres, mudguards, pannier racks front and rear, and pedals with toe clips. Toe clips and straps appeared to have been superseded by special shoes that clip onto little pedals, but as I intended to pedal gently and to be constantly hopping off the bike to inspect castles and suchlike, I decided that normal trainers shoved inside the good old-fashioned toe clips were the thing for me.

When I went for my first ride in trainers, however, I found it to be a very bendy and inefficient pedalling experience, so I turned round after three miles and went home to put on my good old cycling shoes. Their metal cleats and rigid soles make for a far more effective pedalling action, but when you get off the bike you feel like a penguin (or how we perceive penguins, for I imagine that penguins consider their gait to be quite normal) and are in no position to explore castles and suchlike, so I ended up buying some of the new shoes and pedals after all. Technical aside over, save to say that the bike was heavier and slower (mainly due to the stronger wheels and fatter tyres, I think) than my old racing bike, but as I'd be loaded down like a pack horse anyway, speed was never going to be an issue. My new second hand Dawes had a very small front chainring (one of three) and a very large rear sprocket (one of eight) which made the low gears very low indeed, ideal for climbing steep mountain passes effortlessly, or so I thought. Technical aside now definitely over.

As this book is supposed to be about my time in Spain, I need only add that I bought a good saddlebag and set of panniers, stored my car, my effects and few sticks of furniture in a spare outhouse at my uncle's farm, packed, packed the bike into a cardboard bike box, and hit the road to the airport. 'Goodbye, England!' I thought, and still do, for now.

2

When I stepped off the plane that day in early September I realised that summer, at least in Malaga, was far from over, although the pilot having told us that it was 32 degrees there (cheers) some time before landing should have prepared me for it. The heat aside, it felt very liberating to walk across the tarmac, a free man with no responsibilities who could go where he liked and do what he liked for the foreseeable future. I felt slightly less free after I had dragged my bike box off the luggage carousel and put it on my trolley along with my large saddlebag and front and rear pannier bags. I had rejected the idea of a handlebar bag as an effeminate appurtenance (I don't know why, really) that would clutter up the handlebars, and had managed to fit my entire luggage into the five bags quite easily.

After wheeling the lot out of the airport, I found a quiet spot and set about assembling the bike and attaching the bags. Now is as good a time as any to tell you what was in the bags, so I will: cycling clothes, civilian clothes, footwear, a towel, bathroom stuff, a first aid kit, sun cream, maps, a guide book, a small dictionary, a couple of novels, tools, three inner tubes, one spare tyre (folding), spare spokes, spare cables, spare brake blocks, a puncture repair outfit, small front and rear lights (just in case), a camera, a small rucksack, a bike lock, a lightweight sleeping bag and a bivvy bag. Don't imagine that the last two items and the absence of a tent meant that I planned to sleep out in the open every night like a real tough guy. No, it really meant that I had no intention of sleeping out *any* night if I could help it, but that if I arrived exhausted at a place where the inns were full, I wouldn't die of exposure.

I felt that there was little danger of my dying of exposure that first night as I cycled nervously out of the airport and made a beeline for the coastal road into the city which I thought, mistakenly, would not be too busy. The only part of my route that I had planned, and very meticulously at that, was the traversal of the city and my emergence onto the minor road heading roughly north, the A-7000 to be precise, as I had done hardly any research into my general itinerary at all. The trip was intended to be a life-changing adventure, after all, and the problem with carefully planned routes is that you tend to stick to them. What would happen, I thought, if I was sitting on the terrace of a café in, let's say Seville, and I struck up a conversation with a beautiful, dark-haired, almond-eyed beauty who then invited me to her country estate for a few days?

"Sorry, love, I have to be in Carmona by tonight," is hardly what I'd want to reply, is it? 'Sod Carmona,' you might say, but I know myself and remember only too well the teenager (me) who simply *could not* stay an extra night at Malham Youth Hostel, despite the arrival of a minibus full of lithe wee lassies from Stirling, and simply *had to* press on (hiking that time) to Kettlewell, despite the protestations of my pals Paul and Mick, who haven't quite forgiven me to this day, but I digress.

The memory of that hot, sweaty, wobbly, scary ride through the city still lingers and when I had found the A-7000 ('A' for autonomic, or regional, road, rather than 'A' for autopista, or motorway, thank goodness) and climbed a few arduous miles into the countryside, the appearance of a roadside restaurant was most welcome. The sight of a crimson-faced, sweat-soaked individual dressed as, though not feeling like, a cyclist, didn't appear to faze the few men who were standing or sitting up at the bar and who were probably all too familiar with foreign nutcases fleeing the city on two wheels.

After several soft drinks and a snack I decided to make my Spanish speaking debut by asking one of the patrons where I might find a place to sleep that night. The nut-brown, burly chap must have understood me as he removed his toothpick (quaint but true) and informed me that if I continued inland some 30 kilometres I would come to the village of Colmenar, where I would find a selections of hotels and hostels which catered for all tastes and pockets. At least I think that's what he said, as my listening comprehension was still not all that hot, despite having watched Forrest Gump four times in Spanish with English subtitles.

After asking the curiously pale waiter to fill my water bottles, I continued my slow and still slightly wobbly ascent up the sinuous road into a lovely pine forest and reached the top with just enough energy left to enjoy the long descent into Colmenar. There I checked into the first hotel I saw, asked them to put my instrument of torture somewhere out of sight for at least two nights, hauled my luggage up to my room, showered, and collapsed onto the bed for a belated (7pm) siesta.

I'd better point out right now that I do not intend to subject the gracious reader to a blow by blow account of every inch of my route from Malaga to... well, wherever I end up. Although somewhat prone to pedantry in my former life (or so my ex-wife told me, often) I am aware that my mileage, calorie intake, hydration levels, gear ratios, tyre pressures and so on are unlikely to be of interest to the general reader and as this book is more about my interior, or psychological, voyage than my bicycling exploits, I will endeavour to keep the technical stuff to a minimum. I mean, when Don Quixote set off on his horse Rocinante with his faithful Sancho on his donkey, he didn't tell us exactly how many leagues they had ridden each day or precisely what they had for lunch. They rode from one inn to another and things happened, lots of things, and he had profound thoughts, heaps of them, and so it will be with my account, albeit with less conversations on the road as I was cycling alone, apart from the odd exchange of words with passing racers.

On the subject of conversation I will stay, however, as after a curative nap I went down to the hotel restaurant feeling fairly refreshed and, after taking my seat at the bar, ordered a beer and some tapas. There was a football match in progress on the television (surprise, surprise) and most of the tables were occupied by local men watching the match, which was Real Madrid against some other team. I'd promised myself before leaving England that

I would try to have a conversation in Spanish every single day until I felt I had mastered the language, after which I guessed I would converse daily merely for pleasure.

In those early days, however, it was a radical change of habit to go from not speaking to a stranger for weeks on end to striking up a conversation with a new one every single day. We English aren't the most gregarious people on earth and when we drive to work and don't get out much of an evening, our sociability levels can hit rock bottom, mine at least. While my brief exchange with the chap in the roadside restaurant technically exonerated me from further dialogue for one day, I did feel that asking directions, or where I might find to eat or sleep, was always going to be a poor effort. I mean to say, me asking, them answering, and 'adiós amigo' was hardly a recipe for delving into the Spanish psyche. As the football fans at the tables seemed engrossed in the game, I cast a glance to either side of me and found I had the choice of an old timer sipping his wine on my left, or a foreign-looking couple to my right.

After a few sips of beer and a couple of battered squid rings (coated in batter, I mean, not knocked about) I had ascertained that the couple, a few years older than me, were English and that speaking to them would not count. Much as I like most English people, being one of them myself, I wasn't yet feeling terribly homesick and so decided to address the oldie to my left. I knew how to ask 'Do you come here often?' and 'Do you live here?' but I dismissed these obvious, inane and possibly slightly odd openers as unsuitable, before ordering another beer in my best Spanish accent ('*th*erve*th*a' rather than '*s*erve*s*a') in order to buy some time (and slake my thirst).

"It is hot for September, is it not?" I finally asked the man, in Spanish, of course.

"Sí," he replied, before suddenly becoming interested in the match.

Other than tapping him on the shoulder or grabbing his legs and swivelling him round to face me, I saw no way of prolonging our brief exchange, so I applied myself to my food and began to eavesdrop on the English couple. (I was soon to learn that with old men in rural Spain it was usually one thing or the other; they would either completely ignore your salutation, or respond with a quick-fire series of mostly personal questions, followed by an in depth critique of modern agriculture, the contemporary world in general and/or the follies of the today's youth, and at first sight you *never* knew which type they were going to be.)

The English couple, who hailed from somewhere in the south-west, were talking about houses. It appeared that they were on a house hunting expedition and were weighing up the pros and cons of two places they had seen that day. Feeling a bit left out of proceedings after being shunned by the ignorant old buffer and reasoning that all things pertaining to Spain ought to interest me, I decided to tell them that I was house hunting too. Why this idea occurred to me and why I could not just say hello like a normal person, I do not know, but they responded well to my opening gambit and asked me where exactly I was looking.

"Er, well, I'm sort of cycling round trying to find somewhere that I fancy," I seem to recall saying.

"Oh, that's adventurous," said the lady, not, I felt, quite believing me. "We're concentrating on this area now. We were looking nearer to the coast, but there are just *so* many foreigners down there now."

"Ah," I sympathised.

"Can't move for 'em," asserted the husband. (Should I describe them? Would it, given the absurd remark that the wife was about to make expose me to charges of libel? I don't know, so I just won't bother.)

"Yes, we've found out that there's a little English social club here and that'll be quite enough for us," she said. "No need to be falling over them every time you go out. I mean, that's not what you come to live in Spain for, is it?"

"I guess not," I replied. "How are you getting on with the language?"

"Oh, not bad," replied the husband. "We've got some CDs in the car at home. We'll get there eventually."

'Like hell you will,' I thought rather than said. "I'm sure you will," I said rather than thought.

After mutual happy house hunting wishes they left, so I turned to the old man once again, determined to squeeze a few more syllables out of him.

"Who won?" I asked.

"Me importa un pimiento," he replied. (Roughly literal translation: 'It bothers me about as much as a pepper.') So that was that.

I did manage to have a short chat with the young waiter while he chalked up my bill and I asked him what there was to see and do in Colmenar.

"There's a hermitage ('hermita') on a hill at the other side of the village, an old church built over something Arabic and a honey museum that opened a couple of years ago," he replied politely but without excessive enthusiasm.

"What's the honey museum like?" I asked, keen to keep the conversation going.

"Here's a leaflet and a street plan. Take a look tomorrow and let me know what you think," he replied, I think, because he spoke very quickly.

"Thanks, I will!" I replied with an eagerness stemming more from his friendliness and the four bottles of beer than any apicultural enthusiasm.

3

I got up the next day feeling surprisingly sprightly and ate a hearty breakfast of toast with cheese and several kinds of cured sausage slices, which did just as well as the bacon and eggs that my mind and body craved; an association born of bed and breakfast breakfasts, I presume, for I never ate it at home, except occasionally for lunch at the weekend. Before I begin to digress wildly, which I won't, I must point out that today was the day when I bought a thick exercise book in which I began to keep a sort of diary, so after having had to wrack my brains to recall exactly what I did on the first day of my journey (and using a tad of poetic licence in the reconstruction of my short conversations) from today onwards I have my notes to refer to (including the reference to the abovementioned craving for e. and b.). I will strive to sift out the literary chaff and present you with a readable form of the figurative wheat.

Surprised at feeling so sprightly then, I perused my (Michelin – Andalucía) map and found that the previous day I had cycled a grand total of about 60 kilometres, or 37 miles, which sounds even less. This kind of distance, by this time, had become a doddle for me and I put down my near exhaustion on topping the hill before the descent into Colmenar down to the heat, the length of the hill and the weight of my bike, in roughly that order. As a consequence I decided to revise my initial idea of cycling at least 60 miles a day in favour of a figure nearer to 40 until the weather began to cool. Reasons, or excuses, for this decision, apart from the heat, were that I was not out to break any records, that I wished to explore the towns and villages through which I passed and that I wanted to be in reasonably good shape in the evenings in order to continue my conversational crusade.

As I had impulsively checked into the hotel for two nights due to my perceived fatigue, I wasn't going to be cycling anywhere that day, but when I stepped out into the hot sun I thought that spending a day finding my feet and drinking in the atmosphere of (slightly) inland Spain for the first time was a justifiable halt in my cycle tour. I did hope that Colmenar was going to be worth seeing, though, and when I had walked along the modern main road and plunged down into the older part of the village with its white houses and narrow streets I began to enjoy my stroll. I said buenos días to everybody I saw over the age of about fifteen and achieved about a 70% response rate, which I thought wasn't bad, as in England I would have got a similar response rate only by choosing the recipients of my hellos very carefully indeed.

As I began the ascent to the hermitage I asked myself why I suddenly saw fit to greet everybody I met, although I was pleased with myself for doing it, and I conjectured that it was probably because I was already beginning to lose my Anglo-Saxon inhibitions. As I've yet to return to England, though I ought to pay a family visit soon, I can't say if I'll immediately resume being my old insular self or if the ways of my adoptive country will have rubbed off on me. I do know that if I start saying hello to everybody I meet on the street over the age of about fifteen I will probably end up in a police cell.

The hermitage turned out to be a modest whitewashed affair with a little chapel and after admiring the view of the valley below and the high mountains to the east, I headed into the adjacent cemetery hoping to find a garrulous gravedigger to philosophise with. Rather than gravestones marking people's resting places beneath the sod, however, I saw that the vast majority of the departed had been slotted into rectangular niches aboveground which looked like miniature block of flats with plaques instead of windows. I found this a bit macabre as I surmised that the old earth to earth and dust to dust process would be rather difficult to achieve in mid-air and I decided there and then that if I were to end my days on Spanish soil and I couldn't be put *under* Spanish soil, it would be cremation for me every time (well, just the once).

Finding myself alone amid the concrete tombs, I decided to head back down into the village to check out the church that the waiter had mentioned. After fearlessly asking a small child for directions I found myself heading uphill again and soon came to a much larger church than I had expected considering the size of the village. They had evidently been very keen on their religion there over the centuries, although there was nobody around during my visit, and after popping my head inside to admire the airy interior and the fact that they trusted people not to nick anything, I headed off to find the honey museum.

From my fleeting description of the church you will have probably deduced, correctly, that I'm not big on ecclesiastical architecture. No, I was to come across many more churches on my initial cycle tour and although I 'religiously' visited the more interesting ones, don't expect an in depth analysis of them from me. I'm the sort of person who would describe himself as 'spiritual but not religious', but I only say that so as not to seem like a complete heathen, which is what I suppose I really am. The honey museum was more my cup of tea and I spent almost half an hour admiring the apicultural artefacts of old and even bought a pot of local honey which I ended up carting all the way to... my eventual destination. The word colmena, I found out later, means hive, so you can imagine that they have always been busy with their bees in and around the village and, according to my friend the waiter, still are despite the worrying decline of the bee population there and elsewhere.

Call me cynical, but I couldn't help thinking that the honey museum was mainly a ruse to attract tourists to the village as although I got the impression that most of the locals had popped their heads round the door at some point, it wasn't a place where many of them chose to while away their idle hours. Still, as ruses went it was quite an interesting one and I still bring it up in conversation now and again when I can't think of anything else to talk about.

As the time was now after one, I started to think about finding somewhere for a spot of lunch. ('Is he going to talk us through his every movement from dawn to dusk every blooming day?' you might be asking yourself at this point. No, I'm not, but as this was my first full day in Spain you'll just have to bear with me or skip a few pages.) My internet research back home had told me that the thing to do at lunchtime was to find a place where they offered a daily menu (menú del día), so I headed back towards the newer part of the village and, having swapped my stream of indiscriminate buenos días for (incorrectly as it turned out) buenas tardes, I decided to ask the first person who responded where I might eat.

While on the subject of the internet I ought to mention that some friends and work colleagues had urged me to bring a small computer or one of those smartphones with me to enable me to stay online during my travels. This I rejected out of hand as, besides not being a big computer aficionado, I didn't want to be consulting the internet every time I wanted to find something out, like where to have lunch. No, it would be traditional means for me, as I knew that if I could instantly find out everything about everywhere I went, I would make far less conversation (and look a pillock standing on the street prodding away at my device). I'm glad that I was offline for my first months in Spain as the uncertainty made me follow my instincts rather than analysing all my options and, not being an adventurous soul at heart, always choosing the most sensible one, which I think it's safe to say that you will later agree that I did not.

Anyway, I was recommended a nice little place for lunch where a three course meal only cost me €9, after which I returned to the hotel to get out of the sun and enjoy a siesta accompanied by the soothing hum of the air conditioning. Much refreshed by my long nap and inspired by a subsequent perusal of my guide book, I strode out into the evening with a tremendous thirst for conversation and a little beer, before striding straight back into the hotel restaurant to debrief my waiter friend regarding my visit to the honey museum in case I missed him later.

I told Paco, for that was his name, that I had visited the three attractions which he had recommended and that I had found the honey museum very interesting.

"Yes, I went when it opened," he said, polishing glasses with a little white towel. "It is to bring the tourists, really."

"Yes, I know," I replied sagely, as if I weren't one of them. "And do many tourists come here?"

"Some come, but just lately there have been many foreigners coming here to search for houses."

"What do the local people think of that?" I asked.

"If it is a house of theirs they are selling, they are happy."

"Ha, ha," I replied in response to his ironic smile.

"No, but people do not mind now because there are still few foreigners here and most live in the country, but we are aware that in villages nearer the coast there are many, many foreigners and this worries some people."

"Why?" I asked.

"Oh, well, some people are ignorant and do not like progress. Also, in those other villages houses are now more expensive because of the foreigners."

"Ah," I said, wondering if Spanish people said 'Ah' and resolving to listen out for it. "Can you recommend another bar or restaurant with good tapas?" I asked.

"Just along the street towards the village, on the right."

"Gracias."

"De nada." (You're welcome.)

(A note on my dialogue: the reader is not intended to believe that at this early stage my Spanish speech and understanding of it were as correct as my reproduction of conversations suggests, but it would be tiresome (especially for you) if I tried to replicate all the grammatical gaffes which I later found that I had been committing.)

Pleased with our lengthy exchange, I headed out to find the eating place Paco had suggested and there found the usual gathering of blokes spaced out on stools around the large L-shaped bar and a mercifully quiet television. The bar wasn't quite as refined and tourist-oriented as the hotel restaurant and when I asked the pleasant lady behind the bar what there was to eat, she began to reel off an interminable list of tapas. Gratifying though it was that she assumed from the 'fluency' of my speech that I would understand her lightning-fast list of dishes, I had to disappoint her and ask her to repeat them more slowly. As in Forrest Gump and the other films which I had watched in Spanish there was no mention of tapas and in my vocabulary studies I had obviously neglected this area, I repeated five or six of the suggestions which sounded good and sipped my beer until they began to emerge from the large kitchen behind the bar.

The beef in tomato sauce and the chicken wings which arrived first were conventional enough, as was the Russian salad which she served up next, but the rectangular brown slabs covered in an oniony sauce which she then produced were a mystery to me. I found them easiest to digest accompanied by chunks of bread and when she returned with my next dish, which turned out to be tripe (callos), I asked her to repeat the previous tapa's name, which was sangre. Sangre, I then remembered, means blood, congealed in this case, but I stoically finished the plate in the hope that it would increase my blood count in preparation for the morrow's ride.

I've never liked tripe, but with the aid of even larger chunks of bread I was able to get most of the stuff down, before using my potatoes in a spicy sauce and a bottle and a half of beer to take away the taste. After making a mental note to look up and study tapas in my guide book, I surveyed the bar to see if anyone appeared to be in a conversational mood, which nobody did, so I paid up and returned to the hotel restaurant in the hope of finding Paco unburdened by too many customers. (My tip to travellers keen to pick up the language is that if you find a willing talker and listener, stick to him or her like glue, as not all Spaniards, especially in the more touristy areas, are gripped with a burning desire to converse with visitors.)

The night being a Friday, Paco and the other two waiters were busy serving after-dinner coffees and drinks to the several families and couples who occupied most of the tables, so I ordered coffee followed by a glass of brandy and just soaked up the atmosphere, reflecting that you wouldn't find anything like it in England, which is not strictly true since the advent of the (dreadful) family-friendly pubs. After a second glass of brandy and having managed to fight off the urge to buy a cigar (which I had given up) I said goodnight to Paco and trudged upstairs to my room, strangely sleepy despite my long siesta, and made some (barely legible) notes in my new notebook cum diary.

4

The next day being just as hot as the last two, I applied sun cream liberally to the parts of my body which would be exposed before I went down to breakfast, in the hope that it would soak in far enough to protect me before I started sweating it out on the first climb of the day. Disappointed not to find Paco on duty, I requested the middle-aged lady who served me breakfast to say goodbye for me, as I was very grateful for his friendly reception which had made my first stay a pleasant one. At about ten I strapped all my bags onto the bike and headed off around the village to find the road to the Embalse (reservoir) de la Viñuela to the south-east.

I had originally intended to head further east from that point to explore the small villages which the map indicated were perched on a high mountainside, but as I had a feeling that they would be too touristy for my purposes, I decided instead to head north and east from the reservoir to the town of Alhama de Granada, where I was sure to find a bed for the night. Had I had access to the internet, I reflected, I would have known the whole area inside out by now and I was, on the whole, glad that my rather slim guidebook gave only very basic information about this part of Spain. Another reason for heading that way was the hope that the further north I got, the cooler it would become, which I guess if I'd been cycling 100 miles a day might have been the case.

Colmenar, as my first day's ride testified, is quite high up and I was pleased to find that the eleven or twelve miles past the village of Riogordo to the reservoir were mostly downhill. If I'm vague about my mileage it's because I had not installed a cycle computer, fearing that an excess of information regarding distance and speed would make me forget that I was a touring rather than a racing cyclist. On my other bike I had managed to reach average speeds of over 16mph on my later rides and I did not wish to try to emulate this on my fully laden tourer. I did not, in fact, wish to think about speed and distance at all, as straining every sinew to beat my previous day's performance would hardly be conducive to the *interior* journey that I kept reminding myself was the whole point of the exercise.

The road surface was good and the countryside, though a little parched after the summer, was splendid, especially when the reservoir came into view some miles before I reached and rode alongside it for the few miles before I took the turning to Alhama. After a couple more flat miles along the eastern bank of the reservoir the wide but practically empty road began to climb, gently at first, but with increasing steepness on passing the junction to Periana, after which it narrowed considerably and the lack of a central white line might have made me nervous had there been any traffic except for myself and the very occasional car.

The grey shaded area on the map had warned me to expect a stiff climb and the seven or so miles up to the provincial border were very hard work in the increasing heat of the day. As I slogged along in my third lowest gear I reflected that it might have been wiser to set off much earlier, but in that case I would have missed the breakfast whose calories I was now burning fast. The mountain pass wasn't really steep compared to our more abrupt English gradients and I tried to distract myself by looking at the view across to the east, but the heat and the weight of my bike certainly made mad dogs and Englishmen spring to mind as I wiped away the fast-flowing sweat and sun cream.

After a brief rest under the shade of a gnarled olive tree, where I drank a bottle of water and took off my annoying helmet and fastened it to the pannier rack, I plodded on upwards, looking alternately at the approaching gap in the mountains and the tarmac two yards in front of me. It was with great relief that I passed the 'Provincia de Granada' sign and entered the long, narrow village of Ventas de Zafarraya, where I stopped at a petrol station to drink two cans of pop in quick succession and refilled both my water bottles.

As the map told me that it was only about 12 miles to Alhama, and expecting a long downhill equivalent to the hill I had just climbed, I decided to press on to my destination and get myself out of the sun. I set off along the long, straight road and began to realise that I was on an extensive plateau and that the long descent that I was anticipating was unlikely to materialise. I was content with the flat road, however, and the mountain breeze made riding tolerable until the road had the audacity to begin to curve uphill again, luckily not for long, before I crested the rise and was able to freewheel for the first time since the reservoir.

The welcome sight of Alhama soon came into view, with its impressive castle and a view of the Sierra Nevada in the distance, and once in the town I stopped at a bar with a shaded terrace and leant my trusty mount against the wall. My map told me that I had travelled the great distance of 35 miles, but rather than being disappointed by this meagre effort, I just felt relieved to have arrived. Cycling up long mountain passes in over 30 degrees' heat is not a pleasant experience, especially for the unacclimatised, and as I sat there taking in yet more liquid I marvelled at the stamina of professional cyclists, many of whom were at that moment taking part in the three week Tour of Spain in which they would ride over *2000* miles, and rather quickly at that.

On asking the young waiter to recommend a not too expensive hotel, he jotted down a suggestion and gave me directions. Thus it was that before two o'clock I was able to store my bike and forget about it until the next day, for this time I had at least been manly enough not to require two nights' rest before moving on. The hotel was a quaint affair in the old part of town and its attractive patio, complete with hanging vines and creepers, enjoyed a fine view of the huge gorge beside which the town is perched. Alhama is only about twice the size of Colmenar, but the castle, its more imposing buildings and two picturesque squares made it feel much larger. I discovered most of this in the evening, however, as after a shower and a daily menu in a nearby restaurant all I wanted to do was get back to my room and hit the sack.

Much refreshed after a long siesta, I showered again and strode out into the town in search of my first real conversation of the day. After walking up and down a wide avenue I adjourned to a terrace for a drink, where I was served politely and left to my own devices. I was, of course, in civilian dress at this time and with my brown hair, brown eyes and relatively (by English standards) dark skin, I guessed that I wasn't exactly an object of curiosity who everybody would be dying to talk to. Not looking especially foreign, it was only when I opened my mouth that my outsider status revealed itself, but if nobody addressed me, which they didn't, how could I make the local people see that I was a traveller with a burning desire to converse?

Why, you might ask, did I not read a book or something and just relax? Now that I am a veteran of many months in Spain, the next time that I go cycle touring that is indeed what I shall do, but in those early days I think I expected people to queue up to talk to me. As I sat sipping my beer and eating peanuts I reflected that if I'd been in my cycling clothes with my loaded bike beside me someone just *might* have stopped for a chat, but I was hardly going to change and fetch my bike just on the off chance, and before lunch I had felt far too fatigued to utter more than the most basic requests.

I decided that a dinner of tapas eaten at different bars was probably my best bet and in the second hostelry I managed to start a conversation with a young man who was seated beside me at the bar. This I achieved by boldly asking him what people did by way of work in the town and he replied that those who had jobs worked in the country or in shops, restaurants or the administration, but many others, like himself, travelled daily to Granada. He worked at a hotel in the city and I told him that I was thinking of cycling there the next day.

"As soon as you arrive you must find a hotel and ask them to store your bike securely. Then when you go out do not wander around in the Albaicín or other old streets with a big camera or anything else that makes you look like a tourist. There are many thieves at the moment and one must be very careful," was the gist of what he said.

"I will be careful. What is there to see here in Alhama, apart from the castle?"

"The castle is in private hands, but there is an old hospital with a pretty patio and an old jail which you can visit to see old photographs and other things, but the big attraction are the thermal baths just out of town."

"Ah, I read about those in my guidebook," I said. "They were built by the Arabs, I believe."

"First by the Romans and then by the Moors, yes."

"Do you ever go?" I asked.

"Uf," he exclaimed, "not since they started charging 15 or 20 Euros just for a short time in each bath. They are really for the tourists who stay at the big hotel there. I must go now. Enjoy your cycling tomorrow, but in Granada be careful of the traffic and the thieves. Adiós."

"Adiós," I replied, making a mental note of his 'Uf' for future use.

In the third and last of the bars I visited I asked a middle-aged man by my side what there was to do in the town.

"Morirse de asco," he replied, before draining his glass and leaving. I later found that his statement means to bore oneself to tears, or death, so I had clearly not caught the chap in one of his more optimistic moods and I guess he was probably out of work. When I returned to the hotel I saw that a few diners were having coffee and drinks on the patio, so I joined them and ordered a brandy. When the waitress brought my drink I asked her what there was to do in the town.

"Nothing much, apart from the baths. Granada is more interesting."

"Are there not a lot of thieves there?" I asked.

"Thieves? Not so many anymore. The principal thieves in this country are all in the government."

"Vale," (OK, right; pronounced 'va-le') I replied. "Do you think...," I began, but she had begun to walk back inside.

I drank up and went to bed.

5

The following morning after having breakfast at the earliest possible time (9 o'clock) I returned to my room and found myself changing into my cycling gear, which I had washed the previous afternoon and hung on the little balcony to dry. While fastening the velcro straps on my shoes I asked myself if I shouldn't change back into normal clothes and visit the old jail and hospital like a proper tourist. Having already packed my bags I decided to forfeit these delights, but I promised myself that I would call in at the thermal baths on my way out of town. When I passed the road to the baths I found that my legs kept on pedalling and I had soon left the town behind and begun to descend into a country much flatter than any I had seen until then, having also failed to take the turning to Granada.

Had I lost my mind? I don't think so, but as most cyclists will tell you, once you are on your bike (or even *before* you are on your bike, as in my case that morning) you don't want to get off it until you have covered a reasonable distance. Old hospitals, jails and thermal baths could wait for another day and as for Granada, well, after my experience of the traffic in Malaga I didn't feel ready to relive that experience just yet. I plan to visit Granada this year, but I'll go on the bus from where I am now and will spend two or three days exploring the Alhambra and the city's other attractions without the temptation to jump on my bike and head off into the hills.

As I'd missed the turning to Granada I thought I'd better take a peek at my map to see where I was heading and I decided on the spot to ride on northwards to Moraleda de Zafayona and from there straight up to Montefrío, a slightly bigger dot on the map. The road to this first village was comparatively flat and I realised that the extra yard beyond the white lines at the sides of this road and many others were making me feel safe from passing traffic, especially the occasional lorries. Not that I rode within that sometimes quite stony strip of tarmac the whole time, but I knew it was there if I sensed that I needed it. Most of the roads that I know in England, including some quite major ones, don't provide this area of safety, probably due to the sanctity and solidity of the dry stone walls, and the fact that Spanish road planners seem to be given a relatively free hand is a boon to the cyclist.

The morning also felt slightly cooler and, despite the less spectacular scenery of olive groves and cultivated fields, I was enjoying this ride more than the first two, so much so that when I began the short climb up through the outskirts of Moraleda de Zafayona I decided to press on towards Montefrío. After entering the almost adjacent village of Loreto I rode alongside the dual-carriageway towards Granada for about a mile until the road took me over it, along the other side, and back into the village which appeared to have been cut right in half by the major road, so perhaps my friends the road planners had not realised it was there. After leaving the village along a tree-lined road I emerged once again into open country and saw that the narrower road was unlikely to present me with any major climbs during the hour I guessed it would take me to get to Montefrío.

The 15 miles took me a little longer than that as after passing a couple of tiny villages the road began to climb into the hills and when I finally rounded a bend and saw the picturesque little town with its (uniquely) round church and another large one perched on a crag, I was ready for a rest. Having cycled a little over 30 miles in a little under three hours I decided that as it was still only one o'clock I would take the unprecedented step of lunching lightly, seeing the sights, and riding on to Priego, another 23 miles to the north-east.

After a sandwich and several pints of pop and water, the call of the wild, or the road, was once again too strong to resist, so I am slightly ashamed to say that of all the sights in this extremely historical town I only visited the round church (quite big and perfectly round) before heading north on a minor road to Los Agramaderos. From there I turned left towards Almedinilla and soon crossed the 'frontier' into Cordoba province where the olive trees, of which I'd already seen a few thousand, dotted the landscape as far as the eye could see. After skirting Almedinilla I turned onto a wider road and rode the six remaining miles east to Priego with tiring legs but in excellent spirits.

As I refuelled at a petrol stations on the outskirts of the town I consulted my map and calculated that I had ridden a whopping 55 miles in 'only' six hours, including my short lunch stop and brief visit to the round church. Well satisfied by this modest feat I reflected that the cooler weather and absence of mountain passes had made cycling so much more enjoyable and that the more monotonous landscape had bothered me, as the old man in the restaurant had said, about as much as a pepper. Cycling is like that; if you're spinning along nicely on quiet roads you can be just as happy as when riding through spectacular scenery, especially if you're not really up to very long climbs under the burning sun.

After the expense incurred at the relatively plush hotels in Colmenar and Alhama, I decided that I must begin to economise a little, so I asked one of the petrol station attendants to recommend me a cheap place to stay. As Priego is quite a large town (23,000 souls) I'd guessed that not every visitor would be prepared to pay €40 or more for a bed for the night and the 'hostal' that I stayed at was a huge town house with a lovely interior patio where my €22 room, though smaller, was every bit as comfortable as those of the last two hotels and had a television and access to WiFi to boot.

Though I could make no use of the WiFi, I decided to watch TV for a while in order to improve my listening comprehension, but I soon nodded off while viewing a ludicrous soap opera and slept until dusk when I sprang off the bed, massaged some life into my tired legs and hit the town. It seems that practically every town in Andalucía is of historical significance and Priego was no exception. Its main attraction is, however, a natural one, namely the fifty metre cliff which borders the town to the east and which they light up most strikingly at night.

After taking a peek over the cliff and realising that the next morning my desire to put foot to pedal would be greater than my desire to visit the tourist hotspots, I explored the old part of the town with its several water features quite thoroughly before adjourning to a promising looking bar to chat up the locals.

"What is there to see here in Priego?" I asked a grey-bearded bloke at the bar. He responded in great detail to my favourite question and made me feel rather guilty about the fact that I was going to miss most of it. Luckily for me, on winding up his informative spiel, he asked me about myself. I'm not a self-centred person, I assure you, but it *was* nice to be asked and to be able to test my Spanish to the limit by telling the friendly fellow about my reasons for coming to Spain.

After hearing out a potted and probably very ungrammatical account of my thought processes over the last few months, the man nodded approvingly and said that I was a brave man.

"Por qué valiente?" (Why brave?) I asked him.

"Well, because you have cut the ties which fasten most of us to our boring lives," he said, accompanying his speech with some indispensable cutting and fastening gestures. "Not many people are capable of that."

"It's been easy so far," I told him, "but if I don't find something to do, some work to do, in a few months I will have to return to my old life."

"Even so, it will have been a valuable experience, but I think that you will find something to do soon," he said.

"I hope so, but not too soon."

"Ha, ha, yes, work is una desdicha."

"Una desdicha?" I asked.

"Something that makes us unhappy (a misfortune, I later discovered), but, as I said, I feel that soon you will be occupied."

"Why do you say that?"

"Oh, it is a strange thing with me, but I am well known, among my friends, for predicting how things will go for people."

"Really?" I said, his intelligent face convincing me of his sincerity rather than making me suspect that I had come across the town's number one crackpot.

"Yes, your bravery will have its reward," he went on, making me shrug shyly in dismissal of this further reference to my courage, but feeling secretly rather pleased. "You think you are not brave, but listen, I am in a similar position to you, although a few years older. I am a teacher, also divorced and with grown children, and I could easily ask for a sabbatical like you or even retire, but we Spaniards are only adventurous when lack of work makes us go to new countries to earn money. The people of northern Europe are superior in this respect."

"Most of the people I know aren't," I said.

"Ha, ha, no, the majority are the same everywhere. Listen, my name is Agustín."

"Mine is Ken," I said, and we shook hands.

"I will write down my telephone number and I would like very much for you to telephone me in a few weeks to tell me how you are doing."

"I will do that, Agustín," I said, taking the proffered napkin.

"Goodbye and good luck."

"You too," I replied, before watching him light his pipe in the doorway and saunter off down the street.

After this rather intriguing and, it must be said, inspiring conversation I was content to finish my dinner in silence, almost preferring, in fact, not to shatter what seemed like a sort of spell of goodwill that I felt he had cast upon me.

The next morning, as expected, I was keen to make tracks straight after breakfast and I decided to head west towards the town of Cabra before deciding my next move. The weather forecast in the copy of El País newspaper that I leafed through over my toast and coffee told me that the temperature was not due to rise above 28 degrees that day and it was an added bonus to find, once out on the road, that I was to have a healthy tailwind to help me along. After clearing the suburbs where many unfinished houses were in evidence, probably abandoned after the housing bubble had burst some three years earlier, I made good time along the undulating road which soon took me into, but not really over, some higher hills, before I picked up some real speed on the descent towards Cabra.

Unfatigued by my first hour's ride, I stayed on the main road which to my surprise then turned into a pristine dual-carriageway where after a couple of nervous miles spent expecting to hear car horns indicating that a mere cyclist shouldn't even be on such a beautiful thoroughfare, so much like a motorway did it feel, I really got into my wind and gradient assisted stride and wished, for the first and only time, that I'd bought a cycle computer after all. Such was my (sensation of) speed that I left the town of Lucena to my left bereft of my visit and carried on westwards towards Puente Genil, the dual-carriageway having by then turned back into a normal road. A quick stop to look at the map told me that I had about 12 miles to go and it was only on this final stretch that a little tiredness set in and I eased off the 'gas' a little, especially when the outlying factories told me that Puente Genil may not be historic enough to warrant an overnight stay.

When I rode into the centre of town this inkling was confirmed, as apart from a few churches, there didn't seem to be much of interest to see. Accustomed as I was to seeing a castle in practically every town, none of which I had actually visited, I decided to eat a daily menu to replenish the calories that my 45 mile ride at *18 miles per hour* had burnt off. (I confess to being a little disappointed when I later found that Puente Genil was over 500 metres lower than Priego, but no matter.)

Feeling rather full after an €8 feast which made me wonder how they made any profit at all, I trundled out of town at a much slower pace and hoped that the 25 miles that I had valiantly decided to cover to the town of Écija would be as easy as the first part of my day's journey. While the wind still blew in my favour, it now felt distinctly warmer than before lunch and I also soon realised that the undulating road seemed to be rising rather than falling. By the time I reached a little petrol station about two thirds of the way through this final leg I was feeling in much need of liquid refreshment and after purchasing a large bottle of water from an employee who looked as if he had stepped straight out of Cold Comfort Farm, I sat down in the shade of a tree on a little wall and began to drink it.

Some ten minutes later and after I had poured the remainder of the water into my water bottle, I looked up to see a curious sight. Walking down the road I saw a skinny horse, whose hooves didn't seem to clip-clop as loudly as usual, and upon it was seated, bareback, a very brown and sinewy man of about my own age dressed in leather sandals, washed out shorts and a short-sleeved blue shirt that had all seen far, far better days, and for reasons that will soon become clear, a new chapter ought to begin here.

6

Whether it was because my heavily burdened bike told him that I was not from the area, or whether he would have stopped anyway, I can't be sure, but this strange apparition eased his horse round to face me, approached, tugged the reins gently, and slid to the ground.

"Buenas tardes," he said with a smile and in a much clearer voice than most of those I had heard since arriving in Andalucía. "Cycling, I see." His big brown eyes gave me an enquiring look.

"Sí, from Priego today, to Écija," I replied, rather proudly.

"I see you are not Spanish."

"No, English," I said, before deciding to avail myself of this opportunity to speak, despite my tiredness. (I was in no special hurry to get back on the bike anyway.) I told him about my journey so far and that I intended to cycle onwards until I found a place to my liking where I would look for some kind of work.

"So you have no particular destination?" he asked. (Destination in Spanish is destino, which also means destiny or fate, and since that first meeting I have often had cause to wonder which meaning he implied.)

"No, just to find somewhere I like and do something I like doing," I trotted out my well-rehearsed phrase.

"Ah," he said, pushing his rather long hair back and smiling. "It is a good plan."

"Do you think so?"

"All the people I know are slaves to routine, except me."

"What do you do?"

"I live off the land and ignore money as much as possible. Come," he said.

"Where are we going?"

"I will show you my house and my project. It is not far."

"I really must be getting on to Écija," I said.

"Do you have a place to stay there?"

"I will find a hotel."

"You can ring one from the house and I will tell you how to get there. Come," he repeated, before scrambling onto the horse.

Somewhat intrigued and feeling almost certain that he wasn't a mass murderer, I mounted my bike and followed him a short distance down the empty road before he turned left onto a narrow track.

"The country is very fertile here," he said over his shoulder.

"Ah," I replied, supposing that it was.

"Here we are," he said after dismounting in front of a huge metal gate in a high breeze block wall. He pulled back the catch on the unlocked gate and swung one side of it open. He ushered me in and I rode down a short, steep concrete driveway past an ancient Renault Five and squealed to a halt beside the covered terrace of a large two storey house built of the same large grey blocks as the wall. While he was closing the gate I perused the dozen or so skinny cats which were perusing me. He led his sad-looking mount over to a (breeze block) stable with a corrugated roof before striding down the path towards me.

"Something to drink?" he asked, before stamping his foot and shooing the cats elsewhere.

"I've just... well, yes, just a glass of water, please."

"Would you not prefer some herbal tea? It will stimulate you on the rest of your journey."

"Vale, gracias."

"Though it is mostly downhill to Écija from here. Make yourself comfortable," he added, pointing to a motley collection of wicker and plastic chairs around a plastic table, before disappearing through the open front door.

While he prepared the refreshments I surveyed the scene from the east-facing terrace. Beside the wall running alongside the track there were several ramshackle constructions, as well as the more solid little stable, and in front of the house I observed strips of cultivated land descending to an area of fruit trees, beyond which there was another huddle of breeze block edifices which I (rightly) assumed would house livestock of some description. To see the rest of the land I had to step off and away from the terrace and I was viewing a kind of paddock beyond which a high metal fence marked the lower boundary when he came out with a teapot.

"It is a fine view, is it not?" he said.

"Yes, it is," I replied, for if I ignored his ugly grey outhouses, the valley and low hills beyond were charming. When he returned inside for the glasses, teaspoons and sugar I rapidly calculated that the plot measured about fifty by fifty yards and wondered if he could keep body and soul together with that amount of land.

He stirred and then poured out a foul-looking beverage into two small glasses before handing me a teaspoon and pushing the sugar bowl towards me. I noticed that his forearms and hands looked very strong and that his nails were dirty. With two teaspoonfuls of sugar the herbal drink was deliciously refreshing and I told him so.

"A preparation of my mother's, who comes up from Écija to see me occasionally. What do you think of my project?"

"It's a nice piece of land. What is the project about?"

"It is called El Refugio (The Refuge, obviously) and it is for people who wish to step out of the modern, capitalist world and live a natural life."

"How many… members are there?" I asked, intrigued.

"Just one member in residence at the moment, which is me," he said, baring his strong, white teeth as he chuckled briefly, "but several people from the town come up regularly and, who knows, some of them may join me eventually when they tire of their oppressive lives."

"Ah," I said, nodding.

"That is why I built such a large house. My bedroom is downstairs and there are four more bedrooms and a bathroom upstairs. I will show you round when you have finished your drink."

"Did you build all this yourself?"

"Yes, apart from a little help with the roof beams, I built it all on my own. There are some minor details still to finish, but I am much occupied with the land and the animals at the moment."

"Wow," I said, before wondering if they say wow in Spanish. "It must have taken you a long time."

"Just three years. I was obliged to do paid work, in the country, to pay for the materials or I would have finished it more quickly. I built the walls which border three sides of the land first and then the house. I added the stables, chicken house and pigsties after the house and I finished all the building about one year ago, apart from those minor details I mentioned."

(I've said it once and I'll say it again that I'm recreating my conversations from memory and my notes, which I took copiously that night, but his clear voice and considerate choice of words did make him quite easy to understand. My part of this and many future dialogues are 'airbrushed' to say the least, but decreasingly so as my Spanish improved.)

"It's an impressive piece of work," I said. "Will this land be enough when more people join the project?"

"Ha, no, I have some more fields nearby. You will pass them a few minutes after you set off, on your right. I also have a tractor, which is indispensable now, though I hope to plough with horses in the future. Come and see the house."

He led me into a large, tile-floored living room whose walls had simply been whitewashed rather than plastered. On noticing the kitchen area diagonally opposite the metal and glass front door, I realised that the whole ground floor was open-plan, apart from his bedroom, and that it was pleasantly cool inside.

"There is a little bathroom through there and down those stairs there is a large garage," he said from beside the functional but unattractive kitchen area. "Come, I will show you the second floor, all ready for guests."

He led me back across the living area where I saw three wooden easy chairs, an ancient television, an outdated computer, a bookcase and a quirky stone fireplace, before striding rapidly up a steep and very narrow spiral staircase.

"I got this staircase very cheap and it occupies less space," he said with a chuckle as I clambered up the metal corkscrew behind him and emerged onto a breeze block corridor, off which lay the bedrooms and a partially finished bathroom. "One day I will plaster all these walls and it will look much better. Who knows, perhaps one of the future members of the project (el proyecto) will have the necessary skills."

"Well, there's plenty of room up here," I said.

"Enough for the present. In the future I would like people, families perhaps, to build their own ecological homes on my fields, but this is sufficient for now. After you," he added, pointing back down the corridor which I guessed must look much like that of a prison.

After carefully descending the tight staircase, we went out onto the terrace.

"Would you like to see the animals?" he asked.

"I'd really better be getting on to Écija," I said.

"Yes, well, most of the goats are on the other land anyway. Here, apart from the mare, I have three pigs, many chickens, a few turkeys, and one goat which is not very well at the moment."

"Vale. Did you say we could ring a hotel from here?"

"Ah, yes. I only have one number, that of a pensión (hostel or bed and breakfast). It is comfortable and quite cheap." He took an old mobile phone from the fireplace and searched for the number. "A young man from Madrid who came here stayed at this pensión before he arrived, and the night after he left, I think."

"Did he enjoy his stay?"

"He did, at first, but I did not. He thought he was coming to a hippy commune or something and smoked marijuana all day long."

"Ah."

"I am not against natural stimulants, in moderation, but always after the day's work is done."

"So he left?"

"Yes, after five days I told him that I did not think things were working out. Then he said he had no money," he said with a grimace. "I drove him into Écija and lent him €60, which of course he never returned." He shrugged his shoulders and smiled.

"Bad luck."

"Yes, the next time somebody inquires about coming to stay I must be clearer about the nature of the project. When you feel you have cycled around enough you are of course welcome to come to stay for a few days."

"Well, thank you."

"Let's go outside where the phone signal is better. Here you would not need money, except for any luxuries that you require. Here you would have accommodation and I produce almost all of my food. All I ask of guests is that they help me out a little with my tasks."

"Well, yes, who knows, if I come back this way I'd be delighted to come and help you for a while."

"From what you have told me (for I had briefly informed him of the decisions and events leading up to my trip while we were sipping our herbs) you are a person searching for a new kind of life. Perhaps this is the sort of thing that would interest you."

"Yes, perhaps," I said brightly, looking at the half dozen cats which had crept back onto the terrace.

"The phone is ringing," he said, before handing it to me. While I was speaking to an unhappy-sounding woman, he went into the house and by the time I had reserved my room he had re-emerged with a sheet of paper.

"Here is a little map I have drawn. You will see the pensión behind the petrol station."

"Thanks, and thanks for the drink and for showing me round. I'm Ken."

"And I'm Manolo." We shook hands. "I hope to see you again someday. I'm almost always here or on my fields, but I have written my telephone number on the sheet."

"Thanks. You've got a lot of cats," I said, noticing that their numbers were steadily rising.

"Ha, when I had none there were rats, so I encouraged two or three to stay around by feeding them. Since then my mother has always brought food when she comes and there are now far too many. I tell her not to feed them, but she does not listen," he said with a trace of petulance in his voice. "Well, it is an easy ride to Écija," he added more brightly.

"Good. Is there much to see there?"

"Uf! If you like churches, there are many, many churches and also convents. There are some big houses and mansions too, but some are in a bad state of repair. I was born there and my parents live there, but I seldom go unless I have to."

"I will have a look round later."

Manolo bounded up the concrete driveway and opened the gate while I followed more slowly pushing my bike up the short but steep incline.

"Adiós, Manolo."

"Hasta otro día, Ken." ('Until another day, Ken.') "Oh, and just after you pass the Province of Seville sign you will go over a flat bridge. The track on the right after the bridge leads to my fields."

Manolo was partly right about the road to Écija being mostly downhill as, after I had duly looked to the right after the bridge, only to see the usual expanse of olive trees, the road was mostly flat until I reached the final descent towards the town, which lay in a wide, shallow valley and was known, I later discovered, as 'the frying pan of Andalucía', due to the scorching summer temperatures. With the aid of his sketchy map I was able to find my accommodation for the night, a purely functional structure situated, as he had said, behind a petrol station on the main road out towards the Seville dual-carriageway.

Not seeing another entrance other than that of a restaurant, I entered the empty bar area and asked the young waiter if this was the pensión. Without replying, he shouted 'Mamá' (mother) up the stairs, before studiously ignoring me until she came down a few moments later.

"Hola, I just telephoned about a room," I said to the thin woman who looked just as unhappy as she had sounded on the phone.

"It's €20 for one night."

"Shall I pay you now?"

"Sí," she said curtly, so I did.

"Is there somewhere secure to store my bike?"

"You can lock it to the railings outside."

"Er, I'd rather keep it inside somewhere if possible."

"You can keep it in your room if it is not dirty," she said, yet to look me in the eye.

"Vale, I will," I replied, before turning round and going outside.

That was the last time I addressed anybody in the establishment during my stay, as although I'm hardly ever rude, I can be as cold and haughty as the next man when circumstances demand it. After detaching and taking my bags upstairs, I returned for my bike and carried it to my room, which had a fine view of the petrol station and main road. Still, at least it was cheap, I thought, until I saw the official prices on a card behind the door: €16 for single occupancy. After a siesta cut short by the rush hour traffic (7pm in Spain), I showered and set off, intent on discovering a more positive side to Écija.

After wandering down the main road to a dusty park beside the river, I cut through some narrow streets in search of the centre of town. As I was achieving a poor response rate to my cheery holas and buenas tardes, I switched into English mode which, due to the frosty reception I received in the first three bars I visited, I stayed in until the attractive young woman who served me my final tapas of the evening in a bar in the main square, saw fit to make conversation. I told her briefly where I was from and what I was doing and she replied in English that she was Rumanian and that her husband had been an important politician in her home country.

"Écija doesn't seem to be a very friendly place," I said, in English due to the presence of a very morose-looking drunk.

"Here the people are no good," she replied.

"What, here in the town or on the whole area?"

"Just here in Écija. They only think about money and their silly Easter processions. They are also jealous people and liars and hypocrites. They murdered so many of each other during the civil war that they are still neurotic, though perhaps they were just the same before the war too. Another beer?"

"Just a coffee, please. Why are you here then, if you don't mind me asking?"

"Just for the job. My husband wants us to return to Rumania when the political situation is better for him."

(Much later I was informed that the husband was in prison, in Spain, and not for political reasons, so the only friendly face of the whole evening was a liar too, unless the local man who told me was lying due to his innate jealousy and hypocrisy.)

On the long walk back to the pensión I dismissed the peculiar town from my mind and thought about all the positive things that had happened to me so far, especially meeting Agustín and Manolo. I contented myself with the thought that I could always head back this way one day and look them up.

7

The next morning I was awoken at *seven* o'clock by the passing traffic and decided to clear out of the pensión immediately, lest its poor 'feng shui' spoil my day, the first overcast one since I had begun my travels. After coffee and toast in a bar on the other side of the road, I consulted my map before seeking out the road to Palma del Río to the north-east. My intention was to head north from there into the Sierra Morena Mountains which my guide book spoke highly of in a vague sort of way. I had selected my guidebook (which will remain nameless) for its light weight and now wished that I had opted for a more in-depth one, as I was relying mainly on my (excellent, so far) Michelin map to indicate the most attractive roads and villages.

After following the smooth, flat road for a couple of miles a light drizzle began to fall and these unfamiliar weather conditions made me pensive. 'Where are you going?' I asked myself. Up until then I had set off each morning quite content to move on to pastures new, having established no ties to speak of, but as I rode along the damp road through the flat, uninspiring countryside, I remembered

Manolo's invitation to stay for a few days and found myself freewheeling to a halt at the side of the road.

My first train of thought urged me onwards. I had, after all, only been on the road for a few days and there was no reason why I couldn't ride on all the way to Portugal before returning eastwards by a different route. After that, weary of all those miles and the many and varied experiences which would no doubt befall me, I would be more appreciative of a few days' rest at Manolo's before pressing on elsewhere. I clipped my foot into the pedal and pushed off, only to come to another halt some fifty yards down the road.

What, on the other hand, if nothing really happened to me and no opportunities arose during my journey? The cost of each day was already proving to be more expensive than I had anticipated and unless I began to 'rough it' in the cheapest B&Bs and stopped eating all my meals in bars and restaurants, in two months' time I would be a much poorer man than when I had set out. (Up to €4000 poorer, a rough calculation told me.) That way lay ruin before my sabbatical had even ended, I thought, and I would be condemned to relinquish my Spanish odyssey for ever and ever. (I pictured myself in the local pub: 'When I was in Spain…'.) I scooted across the road and faced back towards Écija.

Then again, I thought, it was a bit soon to be hanging up my cycling shoes and if something did come of my stay at Manolo's – through one of his friends or acquaintances, for instance – I might regret not having enjoyed a more thorough tour of southern Spain. Perhaps I should press on for another few days and see what happened? Perhaps I should check out what a stay at Manolo's could lead to now and if there was nothing doing I would be able to rule out that option once and for all? An hour to the east lay a friendly welcome and free accommodation. To the north, west or south lay the unknown. I set off back towards Écija. What, after all, were a few days here or there?

The drizzle soon ceased and apart from the rather long drag out of Écija, the ride back to Manolo's was easy going and at about ten o'clock I was knocking on his high metal gates. On receiving no reply, apart from a few meows, I decided that rather than phone him straight away, I would cycle back to the track he had mentioned and see if I couldn't find him hard at work on his land. That would show initiative and I had a feeling that Manolo would be rather keen on that, possessing a fair amount of it himself.

On leaving the main road, I pedalled cautiously along the untarmaced track which bridged a brook before starting to climb very steeply. Only by engaging my lowest gear and staying firmly in the saddle was I able to avoid spinning my back wheel and I was rather pleased to make it to the top of the short rise, especially when I saw Manolo driving towards me on an old red tractor. He finished the furrow he was ploughing, turned the noisy engine off, and walked briskly towards me.

"Buenos días, Ken. I see you have returned."

"Yes, I thought I'd spend a few days with you now, before I get too far away," I replied, sensing a flaw in my little speech.

"Yes, you cannot stay with me in Galicia, for example, as the project has not yet extended so far." He laughed pleasantly and I was in no doubt that he was happy to see me. "I have two more furrows to plough and then I will show you the rest of my land, down there." He pointed in the direction of Écija. "It goes as far as the stream and some way to the left. I won't be long."

When he had chugged off along the flat field, I wheeled my bike away from the track and leant it against his faded white car. Beyond the field that he was ploughing there were the usual olive trees, but I saw that there were none on the sloping land between the end of the field and the river. When he finished ploughing and joined me, I asked him if he did not like olive trees.

"Pah, olive trees are the easy option. Everybody plants them, as you can see, and they require little work, but the land can offer much more than yet more olives for the cooperative's presses. This long field beside mine belongs to my sister and she, or rather her ex-husband, decided to plant olive trees about three years ago like everybody else. I told her that the land could be much more productive, but she would not listen."

"Ah."

"On the other side of the track you cycled up with your strong legs is my father's land, also mostly olive trees, but he also has some fruit trees and plants vegetables, though less now that he is getting old. That little house there is his, well, his and my mother's, but she no longer goes there."

"Why not? It looks very nice."

"Hmm, they do not get on very well. Not since I was a child, in fact, which is a long time ago now, ha, ha. My father drives her to my house and then picks her up when she has filled all the cats with food." He shook his head sadly. "Here I am going to plant beans and now I will show you what else I have planted and intend to plant."

We walked to the end of the future spud field, but before descending the slope, he stopped.

"Just here I plan to build a large water deposit," he said.

"How will you fill it?" I asked. "Does it rain a lot in winter?"

"Sometimes, but not enough to fill it. No, my idea is to pump water up from the stream. When it is full I will be able to water everything below this level without using the motor. It will be very ecological."

About to become his non-paying guest, I ignored the fundamental flaw in his argument and just nodded. We walked on down the slope.

"This area is a little steep to cultivate, so I intend to plant fruit trees right down to the flat area below. I planted a few plum trees before the summer." He pointed to half a dozen thin, withered trunks. "Unfortunately I did not water them sufficiently. Once the water deposit is built I will lay irrigation tubes all over this area and the trees will grow well. Come."

On reaching the flatter field adjacent to the stream and measuring about 150 by 60 or 70 yards, I saw the first signs of successful cultivation and, near to the reeds alongside the stream, four goats tethered to a makeshift shelter made of pallets.

"Only one of the goats gives me any milk at the moment, but I am hoping that the male goat will soon get active with the other two females." He pointed to a billy goat with patchy hair and a wistful expression. "He looks old, but I was assured that he is still potent by the goatherd who sold him to me."

We both looked doubtfully at the decrepit creature for a while before turning to face the more aesthetically pleasing crops.

"Ah, tomatoes, peppers," I began knowledgeably, "and melons."

"Yes, and water melons too. Over there I planted a little corn and there are also lettuces, broccoli, cabbages, potatoes, onions and garlic."

"How do you water it all? It must get very dry in the summer."

"I pump water directly from the stream with my little petrol engine and it takes me a long time to soak all the rows by connecting the main tube to the little pipes which you can see in each row. When the water deposit is ready I will connect everything and it will be much easier. Now, in fact, the stream is practically dry and this is always a problem towards the end of summer. Even so, I have much more food than I can eat and I give a lot of it away."

"Who to?"

"Oh, to my family and the friends who come up to see me. When more people join the project they will have to visit the supermarket more often as we will have less to spare," he said with a smile. "All this will be picked and cleared soon and then I will plant just potatoes, onions and garlic for the winter. The soil here is among the most fertile in the world and there is a lot of sun all year round, but in winter it can get quite cold at night, so unless I cover everything with horrible plastic I must stick to underground crops in winter. Now I am going to pick a crate of tomatoes and peppers, and milk the goat, but you will want to unpack. Here, take the door key and I will join you in a short while. I think the first bedroom you see when you go up the stairs is the least cluttered, so you can use that one."

"So, is it all right for me to stay for a few days? I haven't even asked."

"Of course, you can stay for a few days or even a few weeks. I am sure a person who can cycle up that hill will be strong enough to help me out a little, ha, ha."

On returning to the house I clicked open the gate, only to be greeted by a cacophony of hungry cats which I picked my way through before leaving my bike on the terrace and opening the front door. I clambered up the squeaky metal staircase and inspected my room. There was a double bed with a dusty bedspread over several blankets and white sheets which appeared, and smelt, clean. The old-fashioned wardrobe was empty and in need of a good dusting, as was the small chest of drawers and rickety bedside table. After wiping my finger on the tiled floor, I decided that I would give the whole room a good going over before I brought up my bags, so I just dug out some shorts, a t-shirt and my espadrilles (which I had yet to see anybody else wearing) and returned upstairs to change.

Two doors along the (dusty) landing lay the bathroom and on closer scrutiny I found that the toilet and sink were in working order, but that the shower was not. There was a sliver of mirror propped up on the sink which I thought might make shaving a perilous affair, so I went down to check out the other bathroom just off the stairs leading down to the garage and found that it possessed a large mirror and functioning shower. I then inspected the kitchen, which I found to be the cleanest part of the house and well stocked with pans and other implements, unlike the fridge which was rather bare. My nosiness increasing by the minute, I went down the stairs to the garage where I found many farm implements, a blue trailer, a washing machine, an old motorbike, two old pushbikes and several large blue plastic cylinders. I screwed the top off one of them and saw that it contained some kind of grain. I then lifted the lid of a large freezer and found it well-stocked with bags of meat and vegetables.

Feeling sure that I would hear Manolo's car returning, I then popped my head round the door of his downstairs bedroom and saw that it was fairly clean but in much disorder. After briefly inspecting a narrow storeroom running down the side of the house adjacent to the track, I went back up the corkscrew stairs and examined the other bedrooms. One contained two single beds and several boxes, while the other two had no beds but many boxes, pieces of old furniture, other assorted clutter and lots of dust. My reconnaissance tour completed, I poured myself a glass of water and adjourned to the terrace to respectfully await my host's return.

After twenty minutes or so and tiring of the cats' meowing, I decided to take a look at the productive animals and after walking through the chickens and turkeys' domain and spotting the skinny goat which stood forlornly in the sun, I made my way over to the pigsty. It was while I was making myself acquainted with the three small but sociable pigs that I heard the car returning, so I walked back up to the house to find Manolo closing the gate and an elderly woman climbing out of the car.

"Ah, Ken, this is my mother. Mamá, this is my English friend Ken who will be staying with me for a while."

"Hola," said his mother, who appeared sprightlier than her wrinkled face suggested. "Staying here for a while, then?"

"Yes, for a few days. I am on a cycle tour," I said, pointing to my still laden bike.

"Uf! Do you not have a car?"

"Yes, but in England."

"It is still too hot for cycling," she said shaking her head. "I rang my son and he told me he had a guest, so I made him come to pick me up immediately. It is not my usual day, but this place is not fit for even pigs to live in."

"I told my mother that we were quite able to clean the upstairs, but she insisted," said Manolo with a shrug of the shoulders.

"Manolo, bring my bags from the car."

"I will get them," I said, before carrying the two heavy canvas bags into the house.

"In the kitchen, please," she said, following me inside. "First I must feed the poor cats. Could you bring me the two plastic bowls from the terrace, please?"

Glad to be of help, I went out to get them and found Manolo sitting in a wicker chair smoking a small pipe. I picked up the bowls.

"Mamá!" he shouted towards the door. "Please do not give the cats so much food. I counted eighteen of them yesterday. They are becoming a nuisance."

"Just a little," she shouted back. "You will starve the poor creatures."

"That is the idea," he said to me. "If I don't feed them, they will go elsewhere."

I took the bowls to the kitchen and returned outside.

"Manolo, tell me where the cleaning things are. I don't want your mother to do that."

"Good idea. She will not be satisfied with your cleaning, but I don't like her to climb those steep stairs too often. I think she is also going to cook today."

"Cook?"

"Yes, she insists on cooking me large stews (guisados) and other dishes, though I tell her I am able to do it myself. She enjoys coming here to get out of the flat in Écija. My father normally brings her and then goes to spend time on his land. I will show you where the bucket and other cleaning things are. Then I have to see to some things around here."

His mother came out with the two bowls brimming with homemade cat food, consisting of pasta cooked with an assortment of leftovers. She laid the bowls on the floor and the cats swarmed round, meowing hysterically until they had fought for their first mouthful. Manolo shook his head, looking truly exasperated, and stalked off through the little gate to the lower part of the land. His mother watched him go and shook her head too.

"If you have cats, you must feed them," she said.

"There are a lot, though."

"Yes, I think there are two more than last week. Sometimes one disappears, killed on the road or poisoned by the neighbours."

"Do the neighbours do that?" I asked.

"I think so. They say the cats damage their crops, but I think it is because they don't like my son's strange ways."

"Strange ways?" I asked, a little worried. She saw my concern.

"Oh, he is a good boy and very kind, in his own way, but he has to do everything differently to everybody else. The people around here are very traditional and don't like change. His land, for example," she began, before making sure he was out of earshot. "He should plant it all with olive trees and in a few years he would make good money."

"But he's planted a lot of vegetables instead," I said in his defence.

"For what?" she asked, raising her hands in exasperation. "He has space here for his own needs and more, but he grows much more and gives it away to those supposed friends of his."

Feeling that she had told me enough for the moment, I resisted the urge to delve more deeply and instead asked her where I would find the cleaning things.

Shortly afterward, armed with dusters and a mop and bucket of soapy water, I walked gingerly up the stairs and set to work. After dusting every horizontal surface, I mopped the bedroom, after which the water was already filthy, so I went downstairs to change it at the outside tap. Three trips later the bedroom, corridor and bathroom were looking much better. I took the bedspread downstairs to shake out the dust and asked Manolo's mother if there was anything I could do.

"First put that thing in the washing machine in the garage. Bring the sheets down too."

"They seem clean."

"The strange boy from Madrid slept in them. He was very pleasant, but seemed sleepy all the time. Bring them down," she said conclusively, so I did.

As she would not allow me to help in the kitchen, I sought out Manolo and found him smoking his pipe on a little wall facing the paddock where the goat stood motionless over a pile of hay that he must have just strewn there.

"So is this goat not very well," I said, stating the obvious.

"No, I bought him in the hope that he would impregnate the she-goats, but from the first day he has got thinner and thinner and I think he will die soon," he said, puffing on the pipe that he hadn't smoked at all the previous day.

"I didn't know you smoked."

"I smoke mostly when I am stressed. My mother stresses me, although she is a very good woman."

"Why does she stress you?" I asked, almost as if I was questioning one of my old customers.

"Oh, now because of the cats, at other times, other things. This goat also bothers me. The goatherd promised me that he was good for at least another couple of years."

"Could you call the vet?"

"Uf! He would charge me at least fifty euros just to come here. The goat only cost sixty. No, we must try him on different food. He no longer eats the hay. In fact, I will tie him up outside the gate so that he can eat the weeds along the wall. He will like those, but first we must catch him."

The gloomy goat made no attempt to escape when Manolo approached him with a noosed rope and after picking up a metal stake on the way up the path, I opened the metal gate and banged the stake into the earth with a rock, close to the wall. Once tethered to a short rope, the goat began to nibble tentatively at the grass and weeds.

"That's better. I should have brought him here earlier, but I have been busy lately. You being here will be a help with all the little things that need doing."

"Yes, anything I can do, just tell me," I replied.

"Now we will take the mare down to the paddock and then I will show you where to find all the eggs," he said more cheerfully.

I'm no expert on horses, but in comparison to those one sees in England, Manolo's mare didn't appear to be bursting with health. Her dark brown coat was distinctly lacklustre and her ribs, if not exactly sticking out, were certainly more visible than they ought to have been. Not wishing to broach the subject now that he had cheered up again, I opened and closed the gates while he led her down the land and into the paddock. After a sniff at the very dry hay and a quick drink of water from a black plastic tub, she ambled over to a makeshift tarpaulin shelter at one end of the paddock and stood there flicking her tail.

"She needs to go out more too," said Manolo, "for exercise and also to eat more fresh grass. Do you ride?"

"Not bareback."

"Ha, no, it is not easy. After I rode her up from Écija I was very sore for a few days."

"You rode her all that way?"

"Yes, for some time I ran a project on some land lent to me by the council. It was intended to get local people interested in agriculture, especially people with handicaps and suchlike. She was very happy there with plenty of space, and grass to eat, but things did not work out, so I brought her here, along with my tractor and many other things."

On seeing his gloominess return, I decided not to question him further on the subject and instead asked him to show me where I would find the eggs. Smiling again, he picked up an old pan from the ground and led me back into the poultry zone.

"They lay mostly in here," he said, entering a narrow, two storey breeze block edifice, empty apart from one brooding hen, which he picked up gently before setting her back down on the egg.

"We must watch out for when the chick hatches and isolate them, or the damn cats will eat it," he said.

We found several eggs in their spacious coop and a few more in various strategic places within their compound. With our haul of eight hen and two turkey eggs, we returned to a house now filled with the smells of cooking.

"You can take these eggs, Mamá, as I have plenty. Is lunch ready yet?"

"Twenty minutes. Hang out the washing, please," she replied while stirring a large pan.

After hanging the sheets and bedspread on a washing line stretched between two of the terrace's brick (not breeze block) pillars, we sat down on the wicker chairs.

"Yes," Manolo said after picking up and putting down his pipe, "it will be a great help if you can assist me with the routine jobs like collecting the eggs, feeding the animals and other little things."

"It will be a pleasure," I replied, wondering how my helping him for a week or two would make any difference in the great scheme of things. "While I'm here you can count on me to help you as much as I can."

"Thank you. Several people come to see me regularly, but they do not really help much. My friend Pepe has placed an advertisement on some online sites for me, inviting people to come to stay for a while."

"What kind of sites?"

"Oh, ecology groups, socialist groups, anarchist groups; anywhere where there might be people who are looking for an alternative life."

"Do you not have the internet here?"

"No, it would be too expensive, and besides, I am not interested in modernity. I want go back to basics and live a natural life. I have no desire to keep up with the latest news and developments in our world which the capitalists are destroying."

"Yes, sometimes no news is good news," I said, translating the phrase as best I could.

"Is that an English expression? I like it. This globalisation is a terrible thing, I think. Soon people will be even more similar than they are already; all thinking about money and possessions and nothing else."

At that moment Manolo's mother emerged with plates and cutlery, so I sprang up to help her. I carried out one of the two large pans from the hob while she brought a stick of bread, glasses and a jug of water. The stew, which contained chickpeas, cabbage, pork, onion, garlic and possibly a few more ingredients, was delicious and the three of us ate in near silence. After a slice of melon for dessert, Manolo went to prepare the coffee.

"What is your job," Manolo's mother asked me.

"My job is helping other people to find jobs," I replied, not knowing the word for adviser.

"Ah, that would be difficult here as there are no jobs at the moment. So you are on holiday?"

"I've taken six months off."

"And they pay you?"

"No, no, but I needed a break. I was getting very tired of it, and of living in England."

"Ah," she said, looking at me for the first time with the tiniest hint of suspicion.

"I've just got divorced, you see, and needed to get away for a while."

"Ah, now I see," she said, my little fib having the desired effect. "Couples don't stick together nowadays, my daughter also separated. Maybe it is for the best," she said with a wistful look, perhaps wishing that divorce had been the thing back in Franco's day. "Manolo, on the other hand," she continued more quietly, "had a nice girlfriend from Madrid and he drove her away."

"Mamá, I can hear you gossiping to Ken," said Manolo, emerging with the coffee tray. "My mother thinks I am crazy not to get a steady job and a steady girlfriend like everybody else," he said to me. "But then I would be a miserable slave like everybody else, too, wouldn't I?" he said to her teasingly.

"Uf, you are impossible," she said, smiling. "Don't make Ken here work too hard, you hear. He needs to rest."

"Work is not hard if you enjoy it. If I was in a factory-"

"Oh, don't start," she said with a dismissive wave. "Let us drink our coffee in peace and enjoy the first cool day for many months."

So that's what we did, and after she had inspected my floor cleaning and I had insisted that I knew how to make my bed, she collected her things – far less of them than when she arrived – and prepared to leave.

"I will see you in a few days, when my husband drives up this way," she said while her son was opening the gates, and then more quietly, "There is a large tupperware in the bottom part of the fridge full of food for the cats. Give it to them in two days when Manolo is not around."

"I will. Adiós."

"Adiós, hijo." (Goodbye, son.)

When Manolo returned half an hour later he said he was going to have a short siesta, so, having already made my bed, put all but one of the blankets in the cupboard, carried my bags up to the room and half unpacked, I did likewise. With the old, metal-framed window open, enough air penetrated the mosquito mesh to cool the grey room somewhat, but, having noticed that the house had a metal corrugated roof, I imagined that things would get hot up in the guest quarters in midsummer. Musing on my conversations with Manolo and his mother, I finally drifted off to sleep and when I awoke almost two hours later I went downstairs to find Manolo's door open, but him nowhere in sight.

I finally located him beyond the stable in a partially walled enclosure amid flourishing tomato plants. The plants he was examining, however, were not tomatoes and, on seeing my surprise, he laughed.

"I grew these from some seeds someone gave me," he said, referring to the three, two foot high cannabis plants. "I sometimes smoke a little before going to bed, as it helps me to sleep. Do you smoke this at all?"

"Oh, not since I was a student, and then only a little. Do the police not worry you?"

"Ha, no, growing a little for one's own use is tolerated nowadays. This one will be ready to dry out soon. What do you plan to do now?"

"I thought you might have some suggestions. Is there anything to do?"

"There are always things to do, but I try to take it easy in the evenings, unless I am engaged in a particular project. I might just turn over the soil around the tomato plants for an hour."

"I will help too then."

"Vale."

He handed me an 'azada' (a large hoe) and went to find another for his own use.

"You start over there and I will start here and we will finish in no time," he said on his return.

I had never used that type of hoe before, being used to the more petite gardening variety, but after watching Manolo thrust his down heartily and lever up the hardened earth, I followed suit and soon got the hang of it. After half a row I took off my t-shirt, but on reaching the end I was pouring with sweat anyway. I saw that Manolo had made more progress more thoroughly and was as dry as a bone. After a little over an hour we met in the middle of a row and downed hoes for the day.

"You are a good worker, but I think you need a shower now," he said, laughing.

"How do people do that all day long in summer?" I asked, examining my already blistering hands.

"Oh, you get used to the work and you get used to the heat, though the heat is bad for everybody, even the Africans who come here now."

"It must be a hard life."

"It is hard but healthy work. Here a man of seventy who has worked the land is normally still quite fit, while a building worker is already in a bad way by the age of fifty, with back problems and suchlike. Physical work is good, but at one's own pace, not the pace set by the exploiters. Let us a have a cool drink."

After my shower I joined Manolo on the terrace and found him less talkative than earlier. While he looked out over the land, lighting his pipe occasionally, I wrote, rather a lot, in my notebook diary.

"Are you a writer?" he asked after another long silence.

"Ha, no, this is a kind of diary. A lot has happened since I left Écija this morning."

"How did you like the town?"

"Not much really."

"Nobody does, except for about half of the Ecijanos. The other half don't like it either. It is good to write a diary. I should write one too. Perhaps one day you will write a book about the success of the project."

"Ha, I doubt it," I replied. "I'm sure it will be a success," I added diplomatically, "but I'm no writer."

8

While I hope that the thorough account of my first day at Manolo's has been informative, if I were to describe each day in as much detail as yesterday, I calculate that the narrative of the second half of my fiftieth year would run to about a million words (War and Peace twice over), so from now on I will *try* to abstain from giving a blow by blow account of every single day and instead restrict myself to describing events of interest in the order in which they happen. Relieved? So am I.

The next day I arose at eight and was surprised to find that Manolo was still in bed, having expected him to have risen with the lark (alondra) and be already digging a trench, pruning a tree, or whatever else farmers do. On reflection, however, and based on what I had seen the previous day, I couldn't think of what there was *to* do, apart from feeding the animals, milking the only milkable goat and collecting the eggs. With a modest set up like this, I thought, there must be plenty of easy days in the year.

Feeling a bit peckish, I opened the fridge and was surprised to see it much fuller than the previous day, and even more surprised that it was mostly capitalist supermarket fare that Manolo's mother had placed there, like cheese, sliced ham, a litre carton of milk, butter, a fruitcake and other bits and pieces. While I was putting a pan on the gas hob to boil some water for tea, I heard stirrings from my host's room and he soon emerged in a white vest and much faded, flowery swimming shorts.

"Buenos días," he said, flexing his well-defined muscles as he yawned. "I see the sky is blue once again today. Did you sleep well?"

"Yes," I said truthfully. "The bed is comfortable, but I needed the blanket."

"Yes, the nights begin to cool off from now on. In winter getting up in the morning can be very cold until the fire is lit."

Feeling sure that his idea of cold and an Englishman's would be very different, and having seen a few logs of wood around the side of the house, I asked him if he lit the fire very often.

"Oh, every day from November to March," he replied. "A stove would be more efficient, but I enjoy watching the fire in the chimney. It helps one to meditate."

"Do you watch television much?"

"No, it is many weeks since I switched it on. I sometimes watch the news, but find the events of the modern world very depressing. What would you like for breakfast?"

"What do you normally have?"

"I usually eat a little toast with olive oil and salt, but there is also butter and jam if you prefer that and even a box of cereals in that cupboard, I think, if you fancy those. My mother insists on buying me supermarket food, although I could do without most of it."

"Yes, I see that there are some new things in the fridge," I said, hoping it wouldn't expose my previous day's prying.

"Oh, my mother is obsessed by food." He sliced a long baguette (or barra de pan) deftly and placed the pieces in the large metal toaster. "It is an obsession typical of people, especially women, of her age in this country. She was born just after the civil war and in this area people went hungry for many years after that, as they did not own the land. She says that the worst hunger is not only being hungry, but wondering if there will be anything to eat the following day. When a woman grows up like that, the need to stuff people with food never leaves her."

"Did you ever go hungry?"

"I don't think so. By the end of the fifties, things were much better."

"The end of the fifties? How old are you then?"

"Not quite so old. How old do you think?"

"About my age, forty-nine, or a little younger?"

"I am fifty-two."

"Really? It must be the healthy lifestyle."

"Yes, and especially the organic food," he said, helping himself to supermarket butter and jam. "I never use pesticides and always feed my animals natural food so that their meat is organic."

I thought about the two elderly billy goats and hoped we wouldn't be eating them when they died, as I have some even older fillings in my molars. There were no tea bags and I reminded myself to get some when we next went into Écija, which reminded me about something I wished to say.

"Manolo, I want to contribute to the expenses of the house. Just tell me how much."

"No, no," he protested, dismissing my mention of filthy lucre with a wave of his hand. "Most of the food is grown on the land and there are very few other expenses."

"I will find a way to contribute," I said, smiling, shaking my finger and beginning to make a mental list which, by the time we had finished our toast and coffee, looked something like this: electricity, gas (large bottles of), rates, petrol, car tax, car insurance, diesel for the tractor, petrol for the water-pumping motor, supermarket food and other products, the (modest) purchase price of (substandard) livestock, tools, farm implements, clothing and footwear, eating out (?) and holidays (?). I wondered how he paid for all this if he didn't do any paid work.

"You look pensive," said Manolo on finishing his toast and lighting his pipe (filled with tobacco, another thing he had to buy).

"Oh, I was just wondering about…" I began, before deciding to limit my enquiries to one specific area, and circumspectly at that. "…what the animals eat?"

"The mare eats hay, grass when I take her out, and a few oats. The chickens and turkeys forage and I also give them a little grain and scraps. The pigs eat grain mixed with water, leftovers and anything else that comes within their reach, including the odd small chicken that gets into their sty. I move the goats about on the land so that they eat the grass and weeds and I also give them hay. The cats I would rather not mention."

"What sort of grain is it?"

"Mostly wheat and corn, and a little barley. I made my own grinding machine which is in the garage."

"So I suppose you have to grow the cereals?" I asked, feeling like the English Inquisition.

"Well, at the moment I am well-stocked with grain. Have you seen the large plastic barrels over there by the stable and in the garage?"

"Yes."

"They all came from the project in Écija that I mentioned. When I was forced to leave I decided that as I had sown and reaped everything practically on my own that the products of my labour belonged to me. I made many, many trips with my little trailer and brought the barrels here, as well as some bales of hay and all the tools and implements which were mostly mine anyway."

I resisted the temptation to ask him why he was forced to leave, but the question floated in the air along with the pipe smoke that he was now producing at a great rate.

"I had to leave because the neighbours on the track leading to the land complained to their friends on the town council that all sorts of undesirable people were going to and fro and that we had a lot of noisy parties."

"Oh."

"Most of the people who came to help or to just sit around were what you might call alternative types and this did not please the conservative, even fascist, neighbours. We only had two parties and just sang a little. Towards the end they threw stones at my car and broke a window. So, anyway, I now have a lot of grain."

"Well that's something."

"Yes," he said with a wry smile, or grimace.

In an attempt to quell my inordinate desire to ask questions, I asked a question.

"What is there to do today?"

"Well, in a while I will show you what the animals normally eat, and after that, well, I was thinking of planting the broad beans (habas)."

"You can count on me."

"Thank you, it will be a great help, especially with the initial watering they must receive, but don't feel that you have to help me all day long. I can already see that you are much more willing than most of my friends who come up here. They prefer to chat and as they have been working hard for their employers, I don't expect them to do much."

"No."

"Only a little if they are to take away food."

"Yes."

"Well," he exclaimed, jumping to his feet. "I will go to the bathroom and in a little while we can begin."

After I had visited *my* bathroom, I descended the stairs and found Manolo waiting outside with a large tin in his hand. After twisting the top off one of the plastic barrels, he showed me how much grain to measure out into the bucket and how much water to add, before leading the way down to the pigsty. The three black porkers anticipated our approach through the little gate to the sty with a chorus of grunts and made short work of their breakfast, before looking up at us like three tongue-tied, porcine Oliver Twists.

"Do you think they are still hungry?" I asked.

"They are always hungry, but they do not grow. If there weren't so many cats, the leftovers my mother brings would be for them. Later I will pick them some apples from the trees behind the house. If the pigs don't eat them, my friends will take them and I think the pigs need them more."

I looked at the too narrow flanks of the chuntering pigs.

"Are you sure there's nothing wrong with them? They might have worms or something."

"Hmm, I don't think so. Here they do not come into contact with other animals, so it is not easy for them to catch anything. Perhaps we should increase their grain by one more tin. Come, let us give the goat and the mare a little hay and check their water, then we can be on our way."

"And the chickens?"

"Oh, yes. On our way back from the land we can cut a capazo full of weeds from outside the gate. Remind me." (A modern capazo is not a basket as the dictionary defines it, but a flexible plastic tub with two handles which comes in various sizes. I was to become very familiar with them.)

The mare didn't look very impressed with the armful of hay that Manolo threw under its nose.

"She doesn't look very hungry," I said, patting her muzzle.

"No. Ha, I know, I will ride her out to the land if you don't mind cycling. I can tie her nearby and she can eat some fresh food."

"Good idea."

"Ha, you are a good influence on me already. I sometimes forget these small details and just rush off in the car."

So it was that I filled my saddlebag with bags of beans and strapped an azada to my pannier rack, while Manolo placed more beans and a large bottle of water in a shabby rucksack and we set off to cover the mile of road and track to the land. As the mare, not looking as pleased as she ought to have about her little outing, was not disposed to trot, I rode on ahead and climbed the steep rise to the field much more easily than the previous day. The lighter bike felt good to ride and I promised myself that in a day or two I would go out for a couple of hours in order not to lose the fitness I had gained. While I waited for Manolo and the mare, I surveyed the field we were to plant with beans. Yesterday it was just a little field, but today we were to cover every inch of it and it now seemed much larger.

When Manolo had finally arrived and tethered the mare by a longish rope to an old fencepost, he took up the azada and we began to plant the first furrow of beans. He scooped aside the loose earth and I popped in the beans at intervals of a little under a foot, after which he covered them with earth. After the first 50 or 60 metre row I stretched my back briefly and we pressed on with the second. After the third row I stretched my back, mopped my brow, drank a little water, and stretched my back some more. After the fifth, seventh and ninth rows, my back stretching, brow mopping and water drinking were becoming increasingly thorough, but Manolo waited patiently while I performed my ritual, even taking a sip of water after the eleventh row.

When we had completed the planting I slumped down on the ground and finished the water.

"We have done that quite quickly," said Manolo from above. "You are a good worker."

"I'm tired now."

"No, when you stand up and walk about you will see that you are not tired."

"Will I? I'll tell you in a few minutes."

After standing up and walking back to the grazing mare I didn't feel so tired after all and I told him so.

"I knew it. You must be fit to ride that bike of yours, but every job uses different muscles. If you planted all day long you would soon get used to it. It is an easy job really."

"Is it?"

"Yes, watering the beans this afternoon will be much harder work. Come, let us go and eat."

After lunching on a different stew (with lentils) from the second large pan that Manolo's mother had prepared, I was disappointed that he didn't head for his room for a siesta. Instead, he loaded the little petrol engine into the boot of the car along with several buckets and capazos, and suggested that we get the watering over with. As his water deposit was still a figment of his imagination, the method for providing water was to station the motor next to a largish pool in the trickling stream and drop a short pipe into it. I looked across the cultivated land and up the slope to the bean field and it seemed a long way away. Manolo then attached the long tube he used to water the vegetables and dragged it to the foot of the slope, before attaching first one and then another hosepipe to the main tube.

"Hmm, if I had brought another hosepipe, we could have reached the field. No matter," he said, but the fifty yards up the slope to the start of the field did matter to me, and that was before we had even started.

Our bean irrigation method was as follows: Manolo would go down to the stream to pull start the motor while I would await the arrival of the water and fill all the recipients. While he walked back up the hill, I would begin to haul a bucket or two up the field and water the area where the beans had been planted. After joining me for one watering trip he would return to the stream to start the motor while I emptied the last buckets onto the beans.

The flaw in this method, as far as I was concerned, was that I was doing two thirds of the lugging and watering while Manolo was strolling up and down the field. After a time I suggested rather astutely that we switch roles for a while, to which he consented. After I had spent five minutes trying to start the dratted motor, he came down to the stream.

"It is difficult to start, isn't it?"

"Yes."

"It is because the original cord broke and we have to use a piece of rope."

"Yes."

"I will show you. You coil the rope tightly and pull, so!" The motor started. "Now you try."

I tried. It didn't start.

"Oh well, we must continue as before."

When we drove back to the house at sunset I wasn't in a talkative mood.

"*Now* you are tired, I think," he said. His smile contained elements of sympathy and amusement in roughly equal measure.

"Yes, I am."

"I must thank you for your help. You can imagine that doing it alone would be very difficult."

"Yes."

"Although with one more hosepipe it would have been much easier."

'Much easier,' were the last words I wrote in my diary in bed that night before falling asleep.

9

The next morning I was very stiff. So stiff, in fact, that I struggled to pull on my espadrilles.

"Buenos días, you have agujetas (stiffness) today, I think," said Manolo when I had lowered myself down the staircase shortly before nine o'clock.

"Yes, I am very stiff."

"And mostly in your legs, I think."

"Yes, my legs are worse."

"I thought so. It is all the bending down when you were planting. It normally happens to people at first. It is a pity that we have no more planting to do just now, so that you could get used to it."

"A great pity." I shuffled across to the kitchen area. "I think today, apart from feeding the animals and collecting the eggs, I won't be of much help."

"No, of course, you must take it easy. It is better to walk a little, though, to get rid of the stiffness."

We had our toast with jam and butter on the terrace, me with the morning sun on my face and Manolo in the shade of a pillar. He hardly needed to sunbathe, but I was keen to tan my skin little by little and it felt good to just sit there, knowing that no heavy work lay ahead.

"What are you going to do this morning, Manolo?"

"Oh, nothing much. I will go out to the land to milk the goat, pick a few tomatoes and peppers and perhaps clear a few weeds."

"Vale," I said, not tempted.

When he had gone, in the car, I collected the eggs, gave the pigs a generous breakfast, and threw some hay down in front of the mare and the goat, neither of whom was much impressed by the offering. As an afterthought I half-filled the grain tin and offered a handful to the mare, which she ate up readily before trying to knock the tin out of my hand. After a few more handfuls I took the tin down to the paddock and found the goat just as appreciative of this dietary supplement, so I refilled the tin and dotted a few fistfuls of the stuff around the poultry compound, causing a minor stampede. Impressed, I took a pinch of grain with the clean fingers of my left hand and ate it.

It didn't taste especially good to me, but I much preferred it to the idea of eating hay, or even weeds, and concluded that the birds and beasts were of the same opinion. While still conscious of the animals' dietary needs, I took a capazo and picked some of the apples that Manolo had mentioned (but not picked) the day before and enjoyed watching the delighted pigs demolish the dozen or so that I threw them, before lobbing one to the goat, provoking the first rapid movement that I'd seen the shabby creature make. I shuffled back to the kitchen for a knife, before giving the mare a quartered apple and cutting the remaining three into small pieces for the fowls.

With my legs slowly coming back to life, I strove to continue the feeding frenzy by tying the goat up outside the gate among the grass and weeds, before moving a little way down the track to pull up a capazo-full of vegetation to share out between the mare and the birds. While engaged in this activity, I perceived a human form out of the corner of my eye and straightened up to see a middle-aged woman standing on the patio of a small house about forty yards down the track in the direction of the road. Her response to my wave and cheery greeting was an almost imperceptible nod of the head, after which she withdrew into her house. Her unfriendliness did nothing to diminish my feeling of wellbeing after putting a little joy, or relief, into the lives of Manolo's animals and for the rest of the morning as I pottered around picking a few weeds and musing, they all appeared to meet my approach with looks of approval and anticipation.

This was the first chance I'd had to do some serious thinking, having spent all my waking hours at 'El Refugio' either in Manolo's company or exhausted, so I decided to take stock of my situation. I sat down on the low wall facing the paddock in the shade of a stunted pine tree and reasoned that the first thing I ought to decide was how long I was going to stay, or at least the minimum length of time I was willing to dedicate to Manolo's project.

One strong argument for sticking around for a while was that I would spend hardly any money and effectively buy myself time. Another was that I would soon be meeting his friends from the town and as Manolo's guest I would be in a position to get to know them properly, rather than just asking my inane tourist questions to everybody I met on the road and hoping for the best. Also, if his friend Pepe had placed an advert online inviting people to stay, somebody might turn up soon (maybe a gorgeous anglophile lady in her late thirties?) to swell the ranks and make life a little more interesting.

Another irrefutable argument was that while I was here my Spanish was bound to improve dramatically, especially if I could persuade people to correct me when I made mistakes, something you could hardly ask of someone you had just met in a bar. Yet another was that I was learning something new, because despite having a farmer uncle, my agricultural knowledge was pretty slim, and gaining the knowhow to become self-sufficient might turn out to be very useful in the future.

The approach of the grizzled goat to the paddock fence reminded me that I was not the only being on the planet and that all my reasons for staying so far were selfish ones: *I* will save money. *I* will meet people. *I* will improve my Spanish. What about these poor animals which Manolo just saw as another string to his bow and didn't appear to have much affection for? I myself confess to not being an animal lover in the true sense of the word. When my children were young, our aging dog, Scamp, became ill and I was faced with the choice of a hefty vet's bill to prolong his life by a few months, or a painless end to his miseries. I opted for the latter, much to the disgust of the kids, and still think my decision was the right one.

'A dog is not a person,' I'd said to my distraught nippers, even adding that they didn't have souls, which hardly helped matters, and I still feel that the English obsession with pets is unhealthy, given all the (human) poverty in the world. Nevertheless, I felt that the poor blighters – Manolo's beasts, not my kids, who can now fend for themselves – deserved a better life. If I looked after them and fed them up for a month, I thought, I might leave him with fatter pigs, more productive egg layers, friskier goats and a horse capable of trotting. Surely then he would see the error of his ways as he waved me off on the road to my next destination, wouldn't he? As for the cats, well, I would have to give a little more thought to that non-productive contingent.

I then moved on to my arguments for cutting short my stay and tootling off within a couple of days. The only one I could think of was that I had set off on a *cycle tour* and that by staying on, though I might become an agile crop planter, I was hardly likely to explore new regions and increase my cycling stamina. I then reminded myself that the modern obsession with sport and fitness had seemed to me like gross self-indulgence until I had pumped up the tyres of my old road bike and got the 'bug' once again. It would be nice to be able to cycle a hundred miles over six mountain passes and get off the bike feeling like I'd just pottered up the high street, but what would I *achieve* by that? I was a pretty unskilled sort of person really and surely now was the time to remedy that, rather than pedalling aimlessly from town to town. In any case, there was nothing to stop me from going out on my bike whenever I felt like it, as my host had clearly stated that my remit was to help him out a bit, not to become his serf.

By the time the cat population had sent a couple of envoys to find out why *they* had been left out of my alimentary improvement plan, I had decided that I would stay for a month. A month would give me time to meet all of Manolo's friends and find out what my prospects were in the area, if any. A month would enable my animal feeding scheme to have an effect tangible enough to convince him that they required, and deserved, more attention. A month would make my first five weeks in Spain very economical ones and perhaps during that time I could find out about other more substantial projects that I could visit.

A month it would be then, I concluded, before returning to the kitchen to take one of the two cat food containers out of the fridge, provoking an invasion of the house. After shooing the feral felines outside with a broom and closing the door, I decided that now was as good a time as any to come up with a cat population reduction scheme. By the time I had had my brainwave, Manolo was fighting his way through the cats and into the house.

"Damn cats! Hello Ken. Oh, I see that my mother has given you instructions to feed the little devils," he said gloomily.

"Yes, but I have a plan."

"Oh?"

"Yes, you will see. I'd like you to take this little saucer of cat food and lure them away down the land before giving it to them. I'm going to put this tub outside the gate and shut it."

"That is your plan?" he asked, scratching his head.

"Yes, they will smell the food, but they will have to climb the wall or get out some other way to reach it. If we start always putting their food, and not too much of it, outside they will stop associating the house with food. If we give them less and less to eat, they will start to look elsewhere."

"Yes, and if they are outside, they will be nearer to the road and more likely to be knocked down," he said with glee.

"That's not what I had in mind, but what do you think of the plan?"

"It is a great plan, but you are forgetting something, or someone."

"Your mother?"

"Exactly."

After a morning spent using my long-neglected initiative, I wasn't going to be put off by this little hitch.

"I will explain my idea to her," I said. "I will also point out that if we can reduce the number of cats, there will be more scraps for the pigs, which need fattening."

"Hmm, perhaps she will listen to you. The point about the pigs is also a good one. When she was young, to have a pig to slaughter was like a dream. When we kill one of them you will see how much of the animal can be used. Almost all of it."

"They need fattening first, though," I said, before telling him that I was prepared to take responsibility for the animals during my stay. "And I will stay for at least a month, if that's all right with you."

"That would be fantastic," he said, looking quite moved. "The animals are not my strong point."

"I'd like to give them all a little more grain, as well as more green stuff and any spare fruit."

"Hmm, there is a lot of grain now, but it will not last forever."

"We can plant wheat when the water deposit is built," I said, forgetting that I probably wouldn't be there for long enough to witness that feat of engineering.

"Yes! We must build it before the spring. Yes, give them grain, of course. Oats would be better for the mare, but I don't have any now."

"When we go into Écija, I will buy some," I found myself saying.

"No, you must not spend your money," he said gravely.

"I insist," I insisted. "When I am cycling I spend up to €80 a day. A few oats is nothing."

"€80 a day! Madre mía, the world is more expensive than I remembered, ha, ha. We will go into town soon and also get those tea bags you wanted. I will buy those."

He then opened the storeroom door behind the staircase and brought out two shallow plastic crates in which he began to place the tomatoes and red and green peppers that he had brought back.

"You picked quite a lot," I said.

"Yes, they were ready. One day soon I will show you how we cook them and conserve them in jars. I will put these bruised tomatoes in a bag for your pigs."

"My pigs?"

"Well, you are their custodian now." He laughed again. "When more people come to the project I think everybody should specialise a little, though of course they ought to know how to do most other things too. Maybe a person who is good at plastering will come one day and help me to finish the inside of the house."

"I'm not very good at that sort of thing," I said truthfully. I had thought that if I was to stay for longer I should at least whitewash my breeze block room like Manolo had done downstairs, but then I'd feel obliged to do the rest of the upstairs rooms, something I didn't fancy at all. Besides, I found the grey colour quite soothing.

After Manolo had lured the cats away with an aperitif, I left their main dish outside the gate and we settled down to partake of the first of Manolo's mother's two stews, which had become even tastier after two days in the fridge.

"This is very tasty," I said. "What is your mother's name, by the way?"

"She is called Eustacia. It sounds strange to say it as I have not heard it used for a long time."

"I might need it when I tell her my plan for the cats," I said, although my main reason for asking was that I was getting tired of writing 'M's mother' in my diary. Now she would become 'E'.

"You might need more than that," said her son. "This afternoon I think I will do some work on my book."

"Your book? What's it about?" I asked, surprised by this revelation.

"It is called El Sistema. It is about what is wrong with the current system and how we can organise society in a better way. It is almost finished now."

"What's your idea for a better society?" I asked, already having a good idea of what he thought wrong with the existing state of things in the modern world; everything.

"Well, I believe we should go back to the land, of course, but I know that most people will not want to do that. I think the way to convince them is to set up a self-sufficient agrarian society in one part of Spain, this area for example, by gradually buying up the land from the capitalist farmers. Eventually we would have our own schools and health centres and try to use money as little as possible."

"Like a state within a state?"

"At first, yes, but as more and more people see that our way of life is better, it will grow and perhaps one day a new country will be formed." His eyes sparkled. "This, El Refugio, is just the first step, of course, but in the book I explain how it can be done."

"Something like Barcelona during the first months of the Civil War?" I asked, remembering the old television documentaries I had watched online.

"In a way, but without the industry. The anarchists made things work well there for a while, but it was a revolution from within established society and the status quo was bound to return sooner or later, especially in a time of war when cooperation was essential. I don't believe the people are ready for a revolution, now less than ever, and my idea is to start something new on the edge of society. You are welcome to read my ·manuscript when it is finished." He laughed and lowered his eyes.

"Yes, I'd like to," I said, perhaps with less fervour than he would have wished.

"Don't worry, it is not a long book and the language is simple. I want people to read it, after all."

"Will you try to find a publisher?"

"Uf! I don't think the establishment will be interested at all. They might even feel threatened."

I conjured up an image of a veteran publisher wetting himself at his desk. "You could publish it yourself. I think that's quite easy nowadays."

"My idea is to publish it myself, here," he said.

"Here? How?"

"By printing out the pages and stitching them together in the traditional way. I have a little book about how to make books that way."

"It will be very time-consuming," I said.

"Ah, something to do on the long winter evenings."

As the temperature was still rising into the high twenties most days and the sun setting well after eight o'clock, it was hard to imagine the coming winter at all, but at that point I was still sure that it would be a very mild affair. After a couple of glasses of *Eustacia's* herbal brew, I offered to take the mare out to pasture. He suggested that I walk past the petrol station where we had met, before turning right onto a track that led down to the river.

"It is easier to mount her by standing on the little wall just down the track," he said when I had put on her bridle and led her out of the stable.

"We'll see," I said, which I didn't, as only ever having mounted a horse twice in my life and over twenty years ago, I didn't feel up to bareback riding, no matter how docile the beast. After a short pit stop at a juicy clump of herbage shortly before reaching the road, we headed past the petrol station, where the attendant greeted me with as little enthusiasm as the neighbour had done that morning, and soon reached the steep track leading down to the tree-lined river.

Although the river had a name, El Río Genil, the flow of water was far from abundant after the summer, but there was lots of lush grass on the shady banks which the mare tucked into with relish. It would have been idyllic down there in the shade of the tall pine trees, had it not been for the profusion of old washing machines, fridges and other discarded goods that people had tipped from the upper part of the track. I counted eleven large items from where I was standing, which wasn't that many, but the difficulty of extracting them from the deep valley meant that they would be there until whoever was responsible for waste disposal arranged their removal, or the end of time, whichever came first.

I seated myself against a tree looking downstream and watched the mare munching away contentedly. From now on, I thought, I would bring her here or take her to the land every day and she would soon get a spring in her step and a bit of gloss back into her coat. Perhaps I would buy a saddle for her if I stayed on after my self-imposed probationary period, although I guessed that Manolo was more likely to have her harnessed to a plough. I reflected that he had reacted well to my offer of caring for the animals and that he did seem eager for me to stay on. How keen I would be after the month was up would depend on the people I met in the meantime, as although he was certainly an intriguing individual, I couldn't see myself living alone with him for any great length of time.

"When do you expect some of your friends to come up to see you?" I asked him later that evening.

"Oh, at the weekend someone is sure to come. What day is it today?"

"Thursday, I think." I looked at my watch to make sure. "One day soon I must go for a ride on my bike. I don't want to lose my fitness altogether," I said, before wondering why I felt I had to make excuses for doing something non-productive.

"Of course. Cycling is like everything else. You must stick at it."

"Have you ever done any sport, Manolo?"

"Not since school. I have always preferred to do constructive things. Not that I think sport is a bad thing, especially for people living in cities and with no other means of exercising, but to play games or run or cycle about has never appealed to me."

"No, I didn't do much for a long time, but I felt good when I started cycling again."

"Yes, we must exercise the body as well as the mind. I'm afraid too many people do neither nowadays."

"Speaking of exercising the mind, can I borrow one of your books?" I asked, pointing to the bookcase.

"Of course. There are more books in my room about all kinds of interesting things. History, politics, economics and so on."

"Oh, my Spanish isn't so good yet." I stood up to look at the shelves behind me. There were many paperbacks of the same collection and I selected one that was not too thick and that I thought I could manage.

"What is that?" he asked. "Ah, El Gran Gatsby, I don't think I have read that one."

"I've read it in English, you see, so that should make it easier."

"Yes, I bought that collection of novels very cheaply at a market some years ago, but I have read very few of them. I find factual books more interesting and useful, though I understand why people need to amuse themselves."

I stood up and returned to the bookcase. "What about this one?"

"Ah, Rebelión en la Granja (Animal Farm) by Orwell. Yes, of course I have read that one. An interesting allegory and his view of communism is probably correct."

"Do you not think much of communism?" I asked, thinking it would be right up his street.

"The idea is good, of course, but most people are too selfish to want to live in such a way. I prefer people to choose for themselves and, if necessary, break away and form a new society, like here, although a society of two is a very small one, ha, ha."

Rather than saying, 'It's a society of one, mate, because I'm only here for the fresh air and the farming,' I just laughed along with him. Shortly afterwards I took myself off to bed.

As I tried to immerse myself in the world of 1920s New York, made difficult by the language and the lack of a bedside lamp, I reflected that Manolo was, all things considered, a pretty odd fish. After three days together he hadn't asked me anything about my past life, whether out of politeness or lack of interest I didn't know, but I guessed that he wouldn't be especially impressed if we ever did get round to talking about it. I was becoming interested in him, though, and I resolved to subtly quiz him regarding his years before he had ended up all alone, apart from me, in his rural refuge.

10

I recall saying earlier that this book could turn into a multi-volume affair if I went into great detail about the events of each and every day, but I see that we are still heading for twice the length of Crime and Punishment before my fiftieth birthday. Put it down to my inexperience as a writer, or to the gripping situation into which I had stumbled, but if I am not to have you flinging the book into the fire before the month is out, I'd better crack on.

Nothing of note happened on Friday and on Saturday morning after attending thoroughly to all my charges I was torn between going out on my bike for a couple of hours or waiting around to see if any of Manolo's mythical friends would show up, something I was loath to miss. In the end I resorted to modern technology and asked him to ring me on my mobile phone if anybody paid him a visit.

"All right, but if it is Luisa with her kids or my old friend Miguel, I wouldn't bother hurrying back as they are not very interesting."

"It doesn't matter who they are," I began, before removing any trace of urgency from my voice lest he suspect me of tiring of his company. "I mean, I'd like to meet them anyway."

"Vale, enjoy your ride."

My legs were still a little stiff when I set off along the road towards Puente Genil, but after a few miles of ups and downs I got into the swing of things and began to enjoy the unfamiliar lightness of the bike, weighed down only by two water bottles, the pump, a spare inner tube and a puncture repair kit. Although the sun was rising in the sky (as it does), the slightly cooler temperature was much appreciated and I trundled happily along the road until I took an impulsive left and headed north towards the small town of La Rambla. The scenery was far from spectacular, olive trees being the foremost feature, but it was a liberating experience to spin the pedals and take in fresh vistas. La Rambla was too ugly to warrant a stop, so I headed east along the smooth, almost flat road towards Santaella, which looked marginally more interesting from the main road, but after riding through the outskirts I decided to press on homeward along the narrow, poorly surfaced, but very quiet road back to Manolo's.

As I rolled down the track I guessed that I had covered about 40 miles during my three hour ride, something that the map later proved to be correct, and I felt so satisfied with my non-productive exertions that I vowed to cycle three times a week from then on. As I leant the bike against the garage door, I saw Manolo approaching, azada in hand.

"How far did you get?" he asked.

I described my route.

"Uf, that is a long way, at least 60 kilometres. I have cycled to Écija and back in the past and that was plenty for me. You must be in very good form."

"Not really, but if I cycle two or three times a week, I will always find the rides enjoyable."

"Yes, I must rely on my work to keep me fit. While you shower I will quickly prepare lunch, because Lola is coming at the coffee hour."

"Who is Lola?"

"Lola is… well, you will see when she arrives."

"I'm intrigued."

While I was finishing my second helping from Eustacia's second stew, the rumble of a car coming down the track was followed by a brutal piece of handbraking and a loud knock on the gate.

"It is open, Lola," shouted Manolo.

"Hola!" sang a short-haired, stocky woman in her fifties dressed in a t-shirt and jeans, after she had slammed the gate shut behind her. "I see you have company for once," she said as she walked down the drive, plastic bag in hand.

"Yes Lola, this is Ken. He is thinking of joining the project."

"Poor man. I am only joking," she said to me, before leaning over and planting a firm kiss on each of my cheeks, the first I had received since arriving in Spain. "You are English, I believe? I saw Manolo's mother yesterday and she told me you had arrived, so I thought I had better come before Manolo frightens you away. You don't look very English. They are normally much paler and have blue eyes."

"I've been in the sun a lot," I replied.

"And you will be in it a lot more if I know this man here, ha! Here," she said, turning to Manolo, who was busy lighting his pipe, "I've brought a bottle of beer and one of cola, so fetch some glasses. So, Ken, tell me about yourself."

"I, well, I was cycling around when I met Manolo and I'm staying for a while."

"Yes, yes, but what do you do? Whereabouts are you from? Are you married? Do you have a family?"

Somewhat stunned by this barrage of questions, but not displeased at being asked, I sketched out the basic details of my provenance, as much for my incurious host's benefit as hers.

"I see, so you are dissatisfied with your life in England and you have come here to start afresh? Beer or cola?" she added before I could answer, as my silent host had just placed three glasses on the table.

"A little beer, please," I said, realising that I hadn't had a proper drink since my evening in Écija.

"It is good to make a new start. I had a brain haemorrhage three years ago and almost died. They thought I was a goner. There was little hope, but I am very strong and I recovered. It made me realise that life is for living, so I stopped working so much – I sew – and started to spend more time with my friends. Isn't that so, Manolo?"

"Yes, Lola," he answered, glass of beer in one hand, pipe in the other and his eyes looking patiently down at the table.

"Manolo thinks I talk too much, but he is always glad when I come, especially when I bring more people, because he is lonely up here all alone."

"I enjoy being alone," he said after finishing his glass and pouring another.

"You think you enjoy it, but you really crave company. Anyway, Ken, are you comfortable here? Do you need anything? Is he making you work too hard?"

Not sure which question to answer first, I just said that I was enjoying my stay so far, earning myself a grateful glance from Manolo.

"You look very fit and I am sure you will help Manolo a lot, but remember that there is more to life than work and insist on having some free time."

"I've been cycling this morning. I'm mainly going to be looking after the animals," I managed to squeeze in.

"Good. Manolo pays no attention to his animals. Where are the cats?"

"Ken has a plan and it seems to be working already," said Manolo from within a cloud of smoke.

"What's your plan?" she asked me.

I outlined my plan and the reasons for it.

"Hmm, I suppose eighteen is a lot. I would take one in, but my doggie wouldn't like it. Oh!" she exclaimed, making us both flinch. "Manolo, do you remember that I told you about the Sahrawi people?"

"Yes."

"Well, I am about to take in a teenage boy for a year. He will live with me and go to school in Écija to improve his Spanish and other subjects."

"That's a big commitment," said Manolo. "Have you met him?"

"Who are the Sahrawi people?" I asked, hoping to keep her on one subject for a while.

"The Sahrawies are from the Western Sahara, to the south of Morocco. After being exploited by the Spanish colonial fascists, they fell straight into the hands of Morocco after Franco died. They fought back for a while, but there has been a ceasefire since, I don't know when exactly, and a lot of them have to live in refugee camps in Algeria. Some of them have Spanish passports and there are a few thousand here, trying to get by as best they can.

This boy that I am going to take in, well, his family live in an overcrowded flat in Marchena and the charity I belong to want to give the youngsters a better chance." She turned to Manolo. "He is called Mohammed, he is fourteen, and, yes, I have met him. For a true person of the left, like myself," she said pointedly, "it is the least I can do to show solidarity with their cause."

"But your flat is quite small," he said.

"It is big enough, and at the weekends he will come here to help you and learn about the countryside."

"Will he?" Manolo asked, meeting her eyes for the first time for a while.

"Yes, it is all desert where he has been living until recently and, let's face it, his only chance of work in Spain when he is older is in agriculture, due to the racism of the ignorant people here. It would be better if he lived here really, as you have plenty of space, but you would have to take him to school every day and pick him up."

"No, no, it is better that he just comes to spend a little time at the weekend," he said, looking as bamboozled by Lola's negotiating skills as I was impressed.

"He is a nice boy and speaks Spanish quite well, although he writes it badly."

"I will show him how to work on the land," said a resigned Manolo.

"Yes, he is quite hyperactive, so a little physical work will be good for him."

"He can also help me with the animals," I said, some of her enthusiasm beginning to rub off on me.

"Good. Now I must go to sew for a while." She drained her glass of cola. "Oh, and another thing, Manolo. Do you remember the couple from the Verdes (Green Party) who came for lunch in the spring?"

"Er, Isabel and…"

"Jorge, yes, well, they want to have a get-together outside the city and I said that you might be happy to let them come here for the day."

"How many people?" he asked with suspicion.

"Oh, no more than eight or ten. They would bring all the food and drink with them from Seville. Isabel says that it is a pity to always meet in the city when the countryside is so important to them."

"All Green Party people?" Manolo asked.

"Yes, all members."

"Well, I suppose it would be interesting to meet them, for Ken also."

"Next Sunday then?"

"What? Oh, yes, all right."

"Mohammed might be with me by then too. I'll see you next Sunday then, at about eleven."

"Do you want some eggs, or some tomatoes?" Manolo asked.

"No, thanks, I still have some eggs from the last time I came. Until next week, then."

"Adiós, Lola," we both said as she scuttled up the drive.

When the car had roared away up the track we both remained silent for a while, recovering our senses. I decided to let Manolo be the first to speak, but before doing so he groaned loudly.

"(Groan) That, you see, is Lola."

"She's very energetic," I said.

"She is a torbellino (whirlwind). She is always enthusiastic about one thing or another, but it sounds like she has committed to something serious with this child. She may regret it," he concluded, pushing his hair back and his beer glass away. "I find her quite tiring."

"Her heart seems to be in the right place."

"Yes, but she expects everybody else to be enthusiastic about the same things as her. I mean, this Moorish child for instance. We don't know if he will have any interest in the countryside. He might want to sit playing on one of those computer devices all day. I wish she would not be so impulsive."

"Well, we (we?) can see what he's like and if he has no interest in the country, you can tell Lola that coming here makes no sense," I said.

"Yes, I shouldn't worry so much and I shouldn't drink beer after lunch. It gives me indigestion. I am happy for the Green Party people to come though. Hopefully they will be interested in the project and will perhaps spread the word."

"Yes, it will be good," I said, probably even keener than him to see these city folk in only eight days' time. I decided to stick my neck out. "I am very eager to meet people, you see, as I've only ever visited Spain on holiday before."

"Yes, not everybody is a solitary as me, but more people will come to visit, you will see."

The following evening, just after I had returned from a spot of rumination down by the river with the mare (grass for her, thoughts for me) a car pulled up on the track and we were soon greeting a very rotund young woman in a pink tracksuit with two kids in tow.

"Luisa, how are you?" asked Manolo with what sounded like forced enthusiasm.

"Oh, so so. I have had better weeks," she replied, puffing out her chubby cheeks and pushing her dyed blonde hair over her ears.

"Let's go to play with the chickens," said the boy of about six to the slightly older girl, who were yet to be introduced.

"DON'T frighten them," screeched their mother, scaring me half to death. "And look for some eggs for Manolo."

As the children disappeared from view beyond the small wooden gate in the poultry fence, I smiled at Luisa, still waiting to be acknowledged.

"So, Manolo," she said, "I see you have an English visitor."

"Yes, this is Ken."

"Does he speak Spanish?"

"Ask him."

"Do you speak Spanish?"

"I try," I said, "but I still have a lot to learn."

"Whoo! You speak very well. I thought English people could not speak Spanish. At the beach they cannot."

"But Ken is not a tourist. He has come here because he is interested in taking part in the project," said Manolo, not, I thought, altogether truthfully.

"What project? Oh, yes, this," she said. "Are you staying long?" she asked me, very slowly.

"For at least a month. I was on a cycling holiday when I met Manolo near here and after chatting for a while he invited me to stay," I said as well and as quickly as I could.

"Ah," she said, nodding thoughtfully. "He speaks good Spanish," she said to Manolo.

While we were engaging in this fascinating exchange, the amount and volume of clucking and squawking had been gradually increasing.

"Pablo! Paloma! Stop playing with the chickens and find some eggs for Manolo!" she screeched over my shoulder. "Yes, this week has not been a good one. I am still feeling quite depressed, but the doctor says to keep taking the same medication. I like to come up here as it relaxes me. Pablo! I will tan your hide if you don't stop chasing them."

I moved my chair slightly out of the firing line. Young Paloma appeared, her pink jacket pockets full of eggs.

"Good girl," Luisa said less shrilly. "Put them in Manolo's fridge and see if there is any cola to drink."

"Take them if you like," said Manolo.

"Yes, I need some. Paloma! Find me an egg box," she shouted into the house.

"Do you want a few tomatoes, or apples?" asked Manolo, fingering his pipe.

"Your apples are too sour, but I will take a few tomatoes, thank you. Is there any tomillo (thyme) or romero (rosemary) in that herb garden of yours?"

"There may be some under the weeds. I haven't paid much attention to it since… for a while," he said.

"Have you heard from Monica?" she asked.

"No."

Luisa stood up and walked around the house, producing a plastic bag from her pocket just before she disappeared from view.

"Is there a herb garden too, then?" I asked, hoping to get the information I desired indirectly.

"Yes, an old girlfriend of mine planted one, but now it is covered in weeds."

"Vale." Seeing that no more information was forthcoming, I went to fetch glasses in which to pour Lola's cola.

Little Pablo soon returned, very heated from his exertions, and after a little more chatter, Luisa stood up to leave with her box of eggs and bags of tomatoes, peppers and herbs.

"I will probably see you next weekend, then," she said as we accompanied them up the drive.

"Yes, but make it Saturday. I may be busy on the land on Sunday."

"OK, adios and, er, goodbye (pronounced 'gudbyee') Ken," she said, laughing at her linguistic skills.

"Goodbye, Luisa."

Not having received an analysis of Luisa after her visit, possibly due to him not wishing to discuss this mysterious ex-girlfriend, I waited until the evening before mentioning her.

"Lola and Luisa are very different, aren't they?"

"Ha, yes. Lola is too much for me sometimes and she tries to interfere here without really doing anything constructive. El Refugio is just one of her hobbies. She has been very left wing since taking part in the demonstrations against Franco's regime when she was very young, but she really has no idea about politics at all."

"And Luisa?"

"Well, she is just a typical townswoman and is probably depressed because of her meaningless life. Her husband, Pablo, is a good man, but he works all the time, so she spends many hours alone in their nice flat, filling her head with the poison that the establishment contaminates simple people with through the television. She used to come along to the old project in Écija and is one of the few people who have stayed in touch."

"She took plenty of food away with her."

"Ha, yes, but I don't mind. Luisa and other people like her need to be taught that the consumer society is not the only way; that there is an alternative. I feel that it is part of my job to educate them, when I get the opportunity."

Rather than pointing out that consumption was never far from her mind on today's visit, I just nodded. "These Green Party people might be interesting, though," I said.

"Yes, the couple who visited once were different from Lola in that they had a good grasp of politics and also some knowledge of agriculture, despite being from the city. Next week we have nothing urgent to do, so I might try to produce an initial version of my book and print a few copies, just on large sheets of paper."

"Is it the sort of thing that would interest them?"

"Definitely. If they take a copy away to read, they might be keen to return to discuss it another day. I will print a copy for you too."

"Yes, I'd like to read it," I said, sincerely, because I wasn't finding El Gran Gatsby as difficult as I had expected and it would be an opportunity to see what made my new friend tick. "Do we not have to do anything to the beans that we planted?"

"They will need more water soon and if God does not help us we must water them once again."

"With an extra hosepipe this time, to get us to the top of the hill."

"Ha, yes. The clever farmer does no more work than he has to."

Manolo yawned, clearly ready for bed, but I couldn't resist one more question before I went up to write my diary.

"You mentioned God just now. Do you believe in him?"

He stifled a yawn. "Oh, I used to be very devout, but not anymore. I will tell you about that some other day."

Yes, and about this mysterious herb-planting ex-girlfriend too, I thought. Manolo's lack of interest in my past life did nothing to diminish my curiosity regarding his, so perhaps I was subconsciously planning this book even then.

11

The next two days were uneventful enough and Manolo's absorption in his 'magnum opus' gave me plenty of spare time, even permitting me to squeeze in another bike ride, around the same circuit, but in the opposite direction. The fact that I shaved ten minutes off my time is neither here nor there, but I did, so I might as well mention it.

Manolo's mother came up on Wednesday morning, just two days after her two stews had given out, forcing us to defrost some pork chops and consume several eggs and many rapidly softening tomatoes until she arrived with her canvas bags and culinary skills. Manolo told me that he had the recipes, but that she was bound to arrive soon and would be disappointed if she weren't able to cook for us.

"She looks forward to her visits and she likes to feel useful," was one of the things that he had said the evening before as he sat in his easy chair, the only one of the three that rocked, surrounded by the sheets that were slowly creeping out of the ancient printer. In his reading glasses he looked quite erudite, almost like a mad professor.

Eustacia lost no time in feeling useful that morning as, after handing me a container of cat food which I managed to sneak up the drive and outside the gate, she began to sweep the living room. Cleaning was a subject that had not arisen and I must confess that it had yet to cross my mind how the downstairs area maintained a semblance of hygiene. As for the upstairs, the breeze block walls made it so dusty that I saw little point in mopping the floor more than once a fortnight. Ever the gentleman, however, I sprang to her side and offered to take over proceedings.

"Ha, men do not know how to clean," she said, a mischievous gleam in her eyes.

"*I* know how to clean," I insisted, "and I can't stand here watching you do it."

"You know how to clean, do you?" she asked, her chin resting on top of the broomstick. (No allusion to witches intended. Eustacia is a lovely Christian woman.)

"Yes."

"And you are looking after the animals, you tell me?"

"Oh, yes."

"Good. That means you will have cleaned out the pigsty already."

"Er, no."

"Manolo!" she called.

"Mamá?" he inquired from the terrace.

"I know that you neglect the animals, but either you or Ken must clean the pigsty. I hate to think what it looks like since I last went down there."

"I'll do it," I said. "It is my job to look after the animals, while I am here."

"When I finish correcting this page," came Manolo's voice from outside, "I will show you how it is done."

After he had connected a hosepipe to a tap situated close to the pigsty, he screwed the end shut and dragged it to the entrance. He then instructed me to first shovel out the bulk of the waste and throw it over the metre high wall of their little patio, from where it could later be used for manuring the land. After that I was to sluice out the sty and sweep the resultant mess out into the patio, which after further sluicing should then be brushed out under the gate.

"First you must change into your oldest shorts and put on a pair of rubber boots which you will find in the garage," he said, before returning to his book editing.

Wellington boots were soon added to my mental shopping list for when we finally went into town, because apart from the fact that the ones Manolo lent me were about two sizes too small, I felt them to be too intimate an item to share, especially sockless. After donning that morning's cycling shorts, which needed washing anyway, I marched back down to the sty with the shovel and a stiff brush and opened the gate, causing the three pigs to scamper away into their bedroom cum bathroom, grunting in a most agitated manner. This was the first time I had penetrated their inner sanctum and the results of probably several weeks of bowel movements was a sight to behold and not one I had fully perceived from the outside, most of the stuff being piled up in the darkest and most discreet corner.

My sense of smell is not very keen, generally speaking, but inside the sty the stench was considerable and it wasn't until I had removed the first shovelfuls that my nausea began to diminish. The pigs soon got used to my presence and became inquisitive enough to join me inside and snuffle at my boots, inhibiting my movements to such an extent that I ejected the ringleader by means of a firm slap on the backside with the shovel. As I worked I wondered how often non-Manolo owned pigsties were cleaned out and concluded that if I performed the task weekly it would be far less onerous than this colossal shit removal operation.

When I had got the concrete floor of the sty clean enough (for them) to eat off, I was brushing away at their patio when I spotted a man coming towards me through the olive trees on the land between El Refugio and the river. He looked like one of your taciturn farmer types, but as he was heading straight for me I thought a greeting was unlikely to be ignored, which it wasn't, but rather than making small talk or asking me who I was, he went straight to the point, as farmers do.

"Those pigs are not fattening," he said.

"No, we've just started giving them more food, and more variety too. I'm Ken and I'm looking after the animals for a few weeks."

"Juan." (Farmer-speak for, 'I'm Juan and I'm delighted to make your acquaintance.') "You can give them all the food in the world and they won't fatten," he said flatly.

"Why is that?"

"They've got parasites in their stomachs."

"How do you know?"

"I just know." The well-fed thirty-something fellow then took a pen and a scrap of paper from his overall pocket and jotted something down. "Get some of this powder and mix it in with their food for a few days. After that they will be fine."

"Thanks, we will."

"Whatever he says," he said, nodding towards the house, "get it."

"Vale."

"Or they will die, eventually."

"Vale. Thanks for the advice."

"(Friendly grunt), adiós."

"Adiós."

After my second shower of the day, more thorough than the first, I left the budding author deep in concentration on the terrace and joined Eustacia in the kitchen. She had finished making the week's cat food and had started on our stews.

"All clean down there now?" she asked.

"Impeccable."

"Good." She lowered her voice. "My son waits until they have no floor left to sleep on before he finds time to clean out the sty. He is useless with the animals and look at him now, sat there like a mad professor." (She said it, I had only thought it.) "What is he reading?"

"A book he is writing. It's about politics, and agriculture too, I think."

"My god, I hope he knows more about politics than agriculture."

"I met a man down there and we were speaking about why the pigs are not getting fatter."

"A young man?"

"Quite young."

"Ah, that will be old Juan's son, Juan. What did he say?"

"That they have parasites and that we should mix a special powder in with their food. He wrote it down for me."

"No matter what my son says, you must get it. Juan and his father are real farmers and they know what they are talking about. Manolo hates to ask for advice, you see, and just goes his own way. He hardly speaks to his father, who has worked the land all his life, and thinks he can find all the answers in books." She shook her head and went on stirring.

I decided to wait until Eustacia had gone before mentioning Juan Jr.'s veterinary advice, but over coffee on the terrace I was waiting for my cue to bring up the subject of my cat reduction scheme.

"Where are the cats?" asked Eustacia at last. "And where is the tray of food?"

"Ah, I have a plan to reduce the number of cats, little by little," I said.

Manolo grinned at me over his coffee glass. His mother looked at me through narrowed eyes.

"For the last few days I have been putting their food outside the gate," I said, before expounding my full theory.

"A dog, or other cats, could get it first," she said in the querulous tone that she normally reserved for her son.

"Mamá, there are no *other* cats. They are *all* other cats, none of them are mine," said Manolo in a voice that threatened to escalate the tension.

"When I put the food out earlier I counted only fourteen cats," I said. "I think being inside the walls was making them lazy, while now they tire of waiting and go elsewhere to search for food."

"Then the rats will come back," was her astute reply. "They used to run across the land over there, even during the day. They were as big as dogs."

"Mamá, you exaggerate. They were no bigger than small cats. Ken is good with animals and, besides, he is in charge of them now."

"Very well," she said. "But when there are less than ten, they ought to eat inside again."

"Three," said Manolo.

"How about six?" I said, using my newly discovered powers of mediation.

"Hmm, we will see," she said, just to me. "But don't forget to put the food I have left cooling on the windowsill into the fridge and then give it to them little by little."

"I will. Soon there will be just a few cats, but healthy ones," I said with a confidence well beyond my few days' experience as an animal guru.

Shortly afterwards a car came to a halt outside the house and after what seemed like a long time the gate opened and an old man stood on the threshold.

"I am here," said an older and more crooked version of Manolo.

"Come down, come down," said Eustacia, a trace of impatience in her voice. "Come and meet Ken."

After he had walked carefully down the drive, I stood up to greet him and proffered my hand, which he shook much more firmly than his tentative gait had led me to expect.

"Hello, I am Ken."

"Buenas tardes," he said, very formally, but looking me straight in the eye and smiling.

"Ken is an animal expert," said his wife, with more than a trace of irony in her voice and a teasing glance at me.

"Are you enjoying your stay?" he asked me.

"Yes, I'm finding it all very interesting."

"I am glad." He turned to his son. "And how are you?"

"Well, and you?"

"I am not bad." He turned to his wife. "Are you ready?"

"Yes, I just need to get my bags."

Eustacia's canvas bags were already packed and a few moments later I had waved them off, closed the gate and rejoined Manolo at the table.

"That was a brief visit," I ventured.

"Yes, my father and I do not have much to say to each other." He lit his pipe. "He is of the same opinion as the other farmers around here who scorn the fact that I farm in a more varied and ecological manner. He thinks that I should plant mostly olive trees and use pesticides like the rest of them. They consider this traditional, but it has only been so since the 1950s. Before that, people managed with only natural, homemade pesticides, such as an aniseed preparation that I use myself, but now they contaminate their crops with all kinds of barbarities. *I* am the traditional farmer, not them."

"Do they think the pesticides are really necessary? I mean, do they work?"

"The problem is that the supermarkets demand perfect produce for their bourgeois customers and anything with the most minimal defect is rejected. I prefer to eat an apple, for example, with some imperfections because then I know it has not been sprayed with poison."

"So did you and your father have big arguments about these matters?"

"Hmm, not really. The big disputes came much earlier, regarding my choice of career and suchlike."

"I see," I said, willing him to go on.

"Now I will go to the land to see if we can soon pick the rest of the summer crops." He stood up. "I would like to plough that part of the land before the end of the month, so that we can plant the potatoes, onions, garlic and perhaps some carrots too."

"I'll come along shortly with the mare."

"Vale."

After fully opening the gates and seeing him off in the car, I put the mare's bridle on, led her out of the stable and we set off. The toot of a car horn and the sight of two youngsters pointing and laughing at me through the rear windscreen made me realise that I must have looked a bit silly walking along with the unprepossessing beast and I resolved to have a go at mounting her once we got to softer ground. For the rest of the twenty minute trip, however, my thoughts turned to my friend's reticence about his past life and I wondered how I could draw him out regarding the girl who had planted the herbs, his controversial career choices, and other events of the fifty years of his life that I knew nothing about.

One tried and tested method would be to get him drunk and as only the presence of Lola had so far made him hit the stuff, albeit a mere two glasses of beer, I thought that Sunday's get-together with her Green Party friends might be a good time to squeeze out some post-party confessions. Then there was the 'weed' planted behind the stable which I assumed he indulged in from time to time. Perhaps I should suggest a spliff or two one evening and hope that it relaxed him enough to lower his guard, although I would have to be careful to inhale as little as possible, as I remember that the main effect it had on me in my student days was to make me fall asleep.

On reaching the track to the land I shelved my intrigues and decided to head up to the bean field rather than cut across the neighbouring olive grove to the streamside plot where Manolo would be. Once up the steep rise that I hoped I was walking for the last time, I stopped on a strip of fallow land near the invisible bean plants in order to practise my horsemanship out of my friend's sight. I then decided that a little pep talk was appropriate in order to prepare the mare for her imminent conversion from rambling companion to mode of transport. I addressed her as Yegua (mare), as she had no other name, and told her that although I probably weighed almost two stone more than her official owner, I would only ride her for as long as she thought fit and that she was to indicate her fatigue or discomfort by simply coming to a halt, rather than by throwing me to the ground.

Horse whispering session over and after a final firm pat on the back, I moved around to her left side and after a brief visualisation of my agile spring, I sprang onto her back agilely enough to fly (well, not quite fly) straight over onto the ground on her other side. After dusting myself down I retrieved the mare, who had walked on a few paces, and after another reassuring pat I tried again, with a little less vim. This time I slithered back down her left flank and it was on the third attempt that I managed to get just the one leg over, before clamping them both firmly against her sides.

I felt pretty lordly up there on her back with the reins in my hands, just like the snooty horse riders back in England minus their awful fluorescent jackets, and their saddles, and I just sat there for a while watching Manolo beavering away down below. When the time came to move forward, however, neither clicking noises, neighing noises, nor lateral pressure with my legs incited her to take a single step. I tried to recall how Manolo had set her back in motion after our first meeting at the petrol station and I thought I remembered him making a noise somewhere between a grunt and a groan which is difficult to write, but I'll try: 'giyuyeee'.

My first grunt/groan had no effect at all and my second slightly deeper one made her step to one side. My third and more protracted effort made her twist her neck in an attempt to look at me (probably wondering what the heck was the matter) and it was only after combining a slightly higher pitched grunt/groan with a firm dig of my feet that she began to walk on. Things went well as she strolled along the edge of the bean field, but when we hit the incline down to the stream I missed a pair of stirrups very much indeed and Manolo later said that the sight of me embracing the mare's neck with my legs flailing around in an attempt to keep my balance was the funniest thing he had seen for a long time.

In an attempt to restore my dignity, I walked her round the large vegetable plot twice, after which a sort of man-mare harmony had been established. As I had forgotten to bring a rope, Manolo suggested leaving her to her own devices by the stream and that her movements would indicate how much she had enjoyed having her first Englishman astride her. I was very pleased to observe that she did not stray far from the spot and I put this down to my innate ability with animals, though Manolo said that she was probably tired out already.

After helping him to pick a large quantity of tomatoes, peppers, onions, cabbages and melons and lugging them up the hill to the car, Yegua and I made the return trip along the road, during which she behaved splendidly, making me feel really pleased that I had begun to ride her. I even envisaged us galloping to the land behind Manolo's car, before I remembered that as she hadn't been shod with horseshoes, it might be too much to ask. Once back beside her stable and still with equine foot care in mind, my exalted state made me brave, or rash, enough to persuade her to lift her feet so that I could inspect her hooves. Manolo told me afterwards that I might have got a nasty kick for my troubles, but the fact that she was quite acquiescent about the inspection seemed to suggest that she was as happy with our new relationship as I was, and to top it all her hooves were fine.

While we ate our supermarket fare sandwiches for dinner, Manolo congratulated me on my horsemanship and also praised my firmness and soundness of argument which seemed to have convinced his mother that my cat reduction scheme was acceptable.

"If I had suggested something similar," he said, "she would have called me cruel and heartless, but then I probably would not have explained it in such a diplomatic way. You have a way with people, and horses, ha, ha."

"I try," I said modestly. "Oh, I forgot to say that I met a man called Juan down by the pigsty this morning."

"Old Juan or young Juan?"

"Young Juan."

"Pah, he is as conservative as his father, if drenching their trees with poison can be called conservative."

"He told me something about the pigs. I suppose he must have been observing them for a while as he wouldn't see them unless he came right up to the fence."

"Yes, that family like to know what everybody else is doing." He lit his pipe.

(An aside: it may seem that my writing, 'He lit his pipe,' every time I want to indicate that Manolo is annoyed is a lazy way of going about things and only marginally better than just saying, 'He was/looked/seemed annoyed,' but I swear that every time he got annoyed, he *did* light his pipe, unless it was out of reach, in which case he would retrieve it and then light it.)

"What did he say about the pigs?"

"He says that they've got parasites. He gave me the name of a powder that we should mix with their food for a few days."

"Hmm, I wonder," he said, seeming to find his wicker chair uncomfortable. "I know the powder he means, of course, and we could get some when we go into town. It is not expensive, so if he is wrong, which he probably is, we won't have lost much."

"I'll put it on my list. When are we going into town?" I asked, wishing that I could have washed the sandwiches down with a nice cool beer.

"Oh, we will go soon. Do we need many things?"

"Well, I need a bedside light and I'd like to get some teabags and perhaps a little beer and wine. Then there are the oats for the mare and the powder for the pigs."

He lit his pipe (honestly, he did). "We will go tomorrow."

12

We will now fast forward to Sunday morning, save to say that we did go into town and bought all the things on the list, including a very cheap bedside lamp at an enormous Chinese bazaar and plenty of beer and wine, which Manolo looked askance at until I told him that we ought to have some to spare in case the Verdes found that the fresh country air made them thirstier than they expected. He insisted on paying for the oats, anti-parasite powder and a pair of larger wellington boots, and when he produced a well-stocked wallet, I once again wondered where he got his money from; yet more information to be prised out of him when conditions were favourable. Apart from a plundering mission by Luisa and her kids on Saturday evening, nothing much else happened until the day of the Green Party get-together.

Feeling good after two more rides on the mare and one on my bike, I was looking forward to the arrival of Lola and the others to brighten up an already very pleasant morning. Manolo also seemed quite enthusiastic about his hosting duties and after we had threaded a few extra chairs down the spiral staircase, we sat on the terrace to await the guests. The yank of a handbrake announced the arrival of Lola at shortly after eleven and a thump on the gate and a shouted request for assistance saw me trotting up the drive with Manolo following at a more leisurely pace.

"Buenos días, Ken. Please help me with these bags."

"Vale. Is young Mohammed not with you?"

"No, he has not come to live with me yet."

As well as several trays of food wrapped in tinfoil, she had also brought many bottles of beer and cola, enough, it seemed to me at the time, for the whole party, as I thought ecologists were earnest, talkative folk who preferred debate to hard drinking. For the next hour Lola bustled and chatted so relentlessly and Manolo smoked so much that it was almost a relief when the well-provisioned convoy of Sevillians arrived and introductions were made. As well as Isabel and Jorge, who Manolo had already met and seemed to like, there were three more couples, a single man and two apparently single women. I shan't describe them all, but their ages ranged from between about thirty and fifty and they were all casually dressed, polite and talkative.

In unfamiliar group situations I always feel a little shy at first and I expected Manolo, living as he did, to be even more inhibited than I was, but this was far from the case. While I stuck by Lola and Isabel, a pretty teacher in her mid-thirties, Manolo mingled like an outdoor lounge lizard, speaking to everybody in turn and offering to show them anything they might be interested in seeing. Isabel's older husband Jorge, also a teacher, joined our little group and informed Lola and I that he had decided to stand as a Green Party candidate at the local elections in Seville.

"I won't get many votes as the Sevillanos could not care less about the environment, but we will be having a little rally in a park there next spring that will be fun and which you must come to."

"I'd love to," I said, keen to take up any excursion opportunities.

"We will be there," said Lola.

"There will be a lot of food and many barrels of beer, so a lot of people will come, ha, ha," he said. "I have to make a little speech after lunch and everybody will applaud as they will be in a good mood by then. In fact, the two or three hundred votes I will probably receive will be those of the partygoers and hardly anybody else, but no matter. It is a good cause and it will be an enjoyable day."

Isabel then asked me about my reasons for being at Manolo's, which I responded to as best I could, not really knowing myself, and I felt drawn towards this pleasant, talkative couple who seemed no more inclined than I was to talk ecology or radical politics. In fact, looking around me, I saw that the main activity, apart from talking noisily, appeared to be drinking large amounts of beer and wine, bottles of which were being produced from the house at a great rate, and eating from the huge buffet we had laid out on every available horizontal surface. (I'd had the foresight to leave a large tray of cat food outside the gate, or we would have had a frenzied feline mob under our feet, meowing for sustenance.) I was pleased to see our host with a glass of wine in his hand and a smile on his face, as happily engaged in small talk as the rest of us. At this point he seemed much less the odd man out than I thought he might be among such a large gathering and I reminded myself that before coming to live alone he might well have led as sociable a life as the rest of us.

Emboldened by three or four glasses of beer, I decided to mingle a little and once attuned to their Sevillian lisps I enjoyed the friendly babble of these carefree folk who had all agreed to leave the kids with their grandparents or other relatives for the day and let their hair down. They had arrived in three cars and as I saw only one person drinking water – a very thin, earnest-looking young woman who my instincts told me to avoid being cornered by – I wondered how they were going to get themselves and their cars back the sixty-odd miles to Seville. When everybody had tired of eating, we wrapped up the excess food which I would later take great delight in giving to the pigs, and Lola prepared two large pots of coffee, which we all sat down to drink around the terrace table and the dining table which Jorge and I had carried out of the house.

A bottle of brandy and many cigarette packets were produced and we all settled down to a spell of post-lunch relaxation. Manolo took advantage of a lull in the conversation to nip inside and reappear with a pile of printed sheets. He laid them on the corner of the table and waited for someone to ask him what they were. The pale, earnest girl obliged, as I had guessed she would, and Manolo rose slowly to his feet, cleared his throat and spoke.

"Er, while we are all seated I would like to tell you about a little book that I have written," he said, provoking murmurs of polite curiosity. "It is called El Sistema and, as its name suggests, it is about the current state of affairs within the capitalist society in which we are forced, some more than others, to live."

Most of the company nodded or grunted their awareness of this sad state of affairs, as they sipped and smoked thoughtfully, and gave him their collective ear.

"The first part of the book which deals with the present situation will not, of course, be news to *us*, but I hope it will inform the more igno-… the less well-informed reader how the powers that be, and I don't mean just the government (tuts and titters), are exploiting their labour."

Out of the corner of my eye I saw how a tall man called Juan stifled a yawn with consummate skill.

"To criticise is easy, of course, so I have not limited myself to explaining just what is wrong, but have also attempted to explain how, in my opinion, the Spanish people could live a far better life. The manuscript still needs a little revision before I begin to bind the books, but I have taken the liberty of printing a few copies to show to interested parties. I have written my phone number on the last page and would be grateful for any comments after you have read it."

"Do we have to read it now?" asked Lola, causing a ripple of laughter which Manolo waited patiently to end.

"No, Lola, today we are enjoying ourselves too much, but in a fortnight or so I will be asking for your opinion, so you had better dust off your reading glasses, ha, ha."

As nobody was fighting towards him to grab a copy, Manolo circled the table, leaving the paper-clipped document in front of each couple and individual. Most of them flicked through the sixty-odd closely printed sheets before folding and storing them in their or their partner's bags, after which the volume of conversation gradually rose to pre-lecture levels.

"I hope they will read it," Manolo said to me a few minutes later.

"I'm sure they will. I mean, they are all interested in alternative ways of life, aren't they?"

"In theory, yes, but at the moment they seem more intent on drinking as much as possible," he replied, as the man called Juan emerged from the house with a bottle of whisky in one hand, a bottle of cola in the other and a bag of ice between his teeth. "I have left your copy on top of the television, by the way."

"Vale. I have almost finished El Gran Gatsby, so I'll start it soon."

After pouring several whisky and colas, Juan approached us.

"Manolo, do you mind if I roll a little joint?"

"Of course not. This is a free society, within these walls at least. I have a little jar of marihuana if you would like to sample some."

"Thank you, but I have a couple already rolled," Juan said, producing two long, rather thick, roll ups and offering one to Manolo.

"Later, perhaps," he replied, which turned out to be about ten minutes later when both joints were circulating freely and being sampled by all except the earnest woman and myself. There was no peer pressure to smoke, but I found myself saying that as I had just given up smoking I feared that the tobacco content of the joints would get me hooked again, though my real reason was to stay alert until after the party broke up.

The party did break up, eventually, but not before the earnest woman, who as the only totally sober person present was finding it hard to stay interested in the increasingly absurd conversations, managed to corner me and chew my ear off about the lamentable state of the world.

"Perhaps Manolo's book will give us all some ideas about how to make it better," I said, trying to sidle away and rejoin the jolly folk.

"I will read it carefully and telephone him when I have finished."

"He will like that."

"And perhaps I will visit again to discuss the book."

"He will like that, too," I said, thinking that he just might when he had returned to his normal self.

After bulging bags of the fruits of Manolo's field had been distributed, we walked out onto the track to see them off. I asked Jorge if he felt fit to drive.

"Oh yes, the motorway is very straight and when we reach the city I will feel fine."

"Take care."

"You too. If you get bored up here in the winter you must come to stay with us in Seville. Lola has our number."

"Thank you, I might do that."

After we had returned to the house which, despite their befuddled state, everybody had helped us to put into some sort of order, Manolo slumped down onto a terrace chair and relit the remnants of a joint.

"That was a good party," he said, slurring his speech ever so slightly.

"Yes, it was."

"I hope they read my book."

"I'm sure they will, but not tonight."

"Ha, no, not tonight." He took a sip from a nearby glass of beer and settled back in the wicker chair.

"So, your girlfriend who planted the herbs, did she live here?"

"Who? Oh, Monica, no, she was living in Écija when we met, but was later sent to Madrid."

"Sent?"

"Yes, she has a good job as a civil servant and has to go wherever she is posted. I suggested that she resign and come to join me here, but she is far too materialistic for that."

"Hmm, it's not easy to pack in a job for life though, is it?" He didn't respond. "I suppose you could have visited her in Madrid."

"I did once, but it was not a success. She had expected me to wear nicer clothes and when she suggested that we go to a restaurant for dinner, I told her that she would have to pay."

"Oh, did you not have much cash?"

"I had plenty, but I refuse to pay for other people to make my food. She didn't understand that and said that I should conform a little. I told her I was too old to start conforming now, he, he."

In his semi-stoned state his laugh had changed, but he seemed forthcoming enough.

"So was she younger than you?"

"Oh, yes, she will be thirty-four or five now. She is a pretty girl, but I could not leave all this and go to the city. I hate cities." He blew a thick cloud of smoke into the air.

"Have you never lived in one?"

"What a lot of question you ask, Ken, he, he. Yes, I studied in Madrid for four years. Even then, when I came home during the holidays – to my father's land, not this, as I bought this much later – I threw myself onto the earth with pleasure and relief."

"Metaphorically speaking?"

"No, literally. It was a kind of ritual for me."

"What did you study in Madrid?"

"Oh, enough questions for now, Ken, as the answer to that one will lead to many more and I am rather sleepy. I will tell you my life story another time, he, he."

"Vale, I'll go to give the pigs some of the leftover food."

When I returned to the terrace just after sundown he had gone to his room, so I finished tidying up before fetching one last bottle of beer. As I sat watching the sky darken I looked back on the day's events and wondered if English Green Party people were as boisterous and intemperate as the Sevillian branch. I appreciated Isabel and Jorge's invitation to stay and filed it away in my mental diary. I wasn't as adverse to cities as Manolo and if I ever chose to settle in Seville, I now knew that I would at least know a few people there.

13

The following week saw a perceptible fattening of all three pigs, of which I informed their owner when I was sure it was not just my imagination. After making a rare visit to the sty he agreed that they had started to put on weight.

"It could be the powder, or it could be just the fact that you have been feeding them a greater variety of food. In either case, I am grateful for your help and I think that in a few months we will be able to kill one of them."

"I won't give them names, then."

"No, it is better not to give animals names, for they are just animals. The only goat which provides milk is called Bambi, by the way, but she was christened by Luisa's children."

"I thought Bambi was a deer?"

"Yes, it shows how much today's children know about animals, but at least Pablo and Paloma are beginning to learn something about them."

"They certainly scare the chickens."

"Ha, Pablo is a little devil, but it is good for them to come to the country. Écija has always been an agricultural town, but as very few local people work in the country now, they might just as well be in New York or Tokyo."

"Who works on the land then?"

"Mostly people from the villages and a lot of immigrants from Morocco, Ecuador and Eastern European countries like Rumania, although after the latest financial crisis more locals have been forced to return to the fields."

"Are you planning to do any work in the country, for someone else, I mean?" I asked, seizing the moment.

"Not if I can help it, although over the Christmas period I normally work as a night watchman at an olive cooperative near Écija. It is three or four weeks' work and it gets me out of most of the holiday celebrations. It also allows me to read a lot, something you cannot do if you are picking olives or fruit as fast as you can."

"So do you get by on just those few weeks' work?"

"Ha, no, I also have my little pension."

"Pension? But you're only fifty-two."

"Yes, that is the age here in Andalucía when one can receive a pension if one has worked in agriculture for a certain number of years. I do not normally celebrate my birthdays, but I had a little retirement party for my last one, ha, ha. However," he said more seriously, "I do not intend to work less than before, but now I can work for myself rather than being exploited by a lazy landowner who counts his profits in the comfort of his city home."

"Yes, a pension is a handy thing to have," I said, feeling rather envious.

"Better conditions were established for the agricultural worker once we joined the European Union. In Andalucía, and Extremadura too, the people were treated like slaves for so many generations that they now have their recompense. There are special unemployment benefits due to the seasonal nature of the work as well as the pension."

"That's good."

"It is good, but not as good as life would be if we adopted my system. Have you started to read my book yet?"

"Er, I've just a few pages of the novel to finish first and then I'll start it."

"I am not as good a writer as…"

"Scott Fitzgerald."

"Yes, but I think my message is more important."

I had told him a little white lie about the book, but I'd found the twenty or so pages I had read so tedious that I realised why all these sportspeople and other celebrities employ ghost writers. His diatribe on the evils of capitalism was dull and predictable to say the least and I hoped that when I got onto the part about his alternative system it would become less mind-numbing. As I was ahead of the game I had also smuggled a Spanish copy of Kipling's Kim up to my room so that at least some of my reading would be pleasurable.

We went out to the land for a few hours most days, Manolo in the car and me on the mare, and collected the rest of the produce from the bottom field, before removing the irrigation tubes and pulling up the plants. I'm sure the tomato plants would have continued to yield for a while longer, but the ones behind the stable were still thriving in their more sheltered position, so our table, and several others, would be well-supplied with them until the cold weather began, which Manolo insisted it would, eventually.

On Saturday afternoon, after an hour of inane chatter, I helped Luisa to carry several bags of plunder to her nearly new car, but there were still many crates of the stuff left. We stacked up the potatoes, onions and garlic in the narrow store room beyond the stairs, after first removing the putrefying remnants of last winter's crop, which explained the strange smell that had sometimes reached my chair in the living room which the cooler evenings had obliged us to withdraw to after darkness had fallen.

"Yes, in summer it becomes too hot to store even potatoes, but you will see that this crop will last us most of the winter," he said, reminding me that my self-imposed probationary month would soon be up.

I had by then settled into this new rhythm of life and as I was managing to keep up my twice or thrice weekly cycle rides, I didn't feel any real urge to return to my solitary and financially draining travels. In almost a month at El Refugio I had spent a total of about €50 and the realisation that I would spend that amount in less than a day on the road increased my desire to stay on. (Twice by then I had offered Eustacia money towards the shopping which either her or Manolo was paying for, but on both occasions I had been firmly rebuffed.)

"I will probably stay until Christmas, at least, if that's all right with you," I said one evening.

"I would be delighted. For me, you are a perfect member of the project. You work hard when there is work to be done and you are as quiet as me, so we do not disturb each other. I hope that when the next new member arrives, he or she will fit in just as well."

I hadn't really thought of myself as a member of anything, but if my stay fuelled his vision of an alternative society, that was fine by me. Lola hadn't called for over a week, though, and I was a little concerned that another drought of visitors was about to begin.

"We haven't seen Lola for a while," I said.

"No, she probably hasn't finished my book yet and doesn't want to come until she is ready to discuss it. Either that or her Sahrawi child is giving her problems, though if that were the case she would be more likely to bring him here, I think, ha, ha."

I thought it more probable that she hadn't even got beyond the first page of the tiresome manuscript, but didn't say so.

"Who else usually visits?" I asked.

"Well, there is Miguel, who I used to work with in the country, and Pepe, who is a very old friend and something of a poet, but he sometimes has periods of depression and does not come for a while."

"You could ring him."

"It would make no difference. He will come when he is ready, though I might ring him to see if he remembered to place the advertisement, online, as he calls it, inviting more people to visit the project."

"What are we going to do with all these tomatoes and peppers?" I asked, not wishing to appear too dissatisfied with his company.

"Hmm, there are a lot. Tomorrow I will fry the tomatoes and sterilise the jars in which we will conserve them. I think I will ask my mother to take the peppers and conserve them at home. It will give her something to do as she gets bored in the flat."

"Does she not see many people?"

"A few, and my sister visits her quite often."

"I didn't know you had a sister," I said, a little miffed that he hadn't seen fit to mention her.

"Yes, Susana. She is a few years younger than me and has a teenage son. She had a lot of problems with her stupid husband –

the one who insisted on planting olive trees and who she has now separated from – so I have not seen her for a while."

"Invite her up one day."

"Yes, I should do. She is not like me, I mean, she is not interested in what I am doing here and she lives the typical life of a victim of capitalism. She works in a factory and then spends the little money she earns there on unnecessary things. She is the perfect proletarian; she works, consumes, works, consumes, and thinks that is normal."

"I suppose it is for most people."

"Yes, but most people do not have an elder brother who has tried to instruct her and make her see the futility of her life. She has as much land as me – our parents split their terrain into three parts some years ago – and I offered to help her to build a little house there and show her how to live off the land. She just laughed and said that I was crazy."

"But, Manolo, did she ever throw herself to the earth after being away from it for a while?"

"No. What do you mean?"

"I mean that most people, including myself until now, have become so divorced from the land that it does seem a little crazy to renounce money (apart from your handy little pension, I thought) and live like a peasant again."

"I know, I know, but I will ring her, and Pepe too, as you might be a good influence on them. Pepe, for instance, is about fifty and works just enough days in the country to get the agricultural unemployment benefit for the rest of the year. He lives with his old mother, although the house is now his, and there is nothing to stop *him* from spending more time here. *And* I know for a fact that when he works he is less depressed, despite complaining about having to get up before sunrise, so there is a direct relation between idleness and depression, as can be seen in the case of Luisa, whose husband is too proud to let her go out to work," he said, getting quite excited.

"What makes you think that I'm a good influence?" I asked, laughing in my most self-effacing manner.

"Because you are less radical than myself. You see both sides of the argument and the fact that you are here proves that it is not madness to live in this way."

"Yes, but I have a job to go back to in a few months if I choose to. I haven't taken any risks or made any great sacrifice to be here."

"Exactly. You have shown that a supposedly normal person, if such a person exists, can participate in a project like this without people accusing him of irrational behaviour. You are a role model for other people," he concluded, lighting his pipe to calm himself down.

"Well, ring your sister and Pepe and I'll see if I can work my magic on them."

"I will, soon. Tomorrow we must water the beans if it does not rain."

14

As if by magic it rained that night and part of the next morning; not much, but enough to postpone the bucket hauling that I had not been looking forward to. Instead we spent the morning chopping up and frying huge quantities of tomatoes with garlic, salt and sugar, before adding herbs and pouring the resultant mush into the sterilised jars we had prepared earlier. Once filled right to the top and with a few drops of olive oil for good measure, we screwed on the sterilised tops and boiled them upside down for half an hour to seal them, Manolo assured me, hermetically. When I put it so succinctly it sounds like a quick process, but it took us all morning and part of the afternoon to produce the thirty-two jars which were an essential ingredient of Eustacia's famous stews.

When I returned from my ride down to the river on the mare, who I thought was looking healthier and happier but still refused to trot, I was pleased to see an unknown hatchback car parked outside. Seated on the terrace was a slim, bespectacled man with thinning hair and a prominent forehead, dressed quite smartly in a checked shirt and creased trousers, the first (ironed) crease I had seen for some time. I waved before guiding Yegua into her stable and walking down to greet him. The almost schoolmasterly chap stood as I approached and held out his hand.

"Hello, Ken, I am Pepe, a friend of Benítez," he said in an even clearer voice than Manolo's.

"Benítez? Oh, is that his surname? I didn't know it."

"He has just gone to milk the goat as he feared that she might explode."

"Ah, that is something I must learn how to do because I'm looking after the animals, while I'm here."

"The animals will be giving thanks to God for your arrival. Are you staying at Manolo's bunker (sic), as I like to call it, for long?"

"Well, until Christmas at least."

"So you must be enjoying this rudimentary lifestyle," he said, smiling with his eyes alone.

"Yes, so far it has been interesting," I replied, before giving my ever-shortening explanation of how I came to be there.

"Good, so you will be able to go back to your job in the spring after having an… illuminating experience." His delivery was very flat, but I could already perceive the dry humour with which he injected most of his statements.

"I might, I suppose, but I might stay in Spain. We will see."

"Yes, Spain has an attraction for English people. I wish I could say it had the same attraction for me."

"You don't like it?"

"As a concept, yes, but life is very difficult here at the moment for a man with no special skills."

"Ah," I said, surprised at such a statement from so articulate a man, but thinking it a little early in our prospective friendship for too much probing. "Would you like a beer or something?"

"Yes, please. I have brought my usual litre of beer as the fridge is usually lacking in liquid refreshments, but I see that it is unusually well-stocked."

"Yes, I bought some and some people came up from Seville last week and left quite a lot."

"From Seville?"

"Yes, some of Lola's friends."

"Ah, Lola, that pseudo-radical talking machine. I cannot abide that woman's empty chatter and try to avoid her. I'll get the beer."

Surprised by the sudden revelation of this censorious side to his character, I used his brief absence to ponder how I could make the most of the short time that we would remain alone.

"Have you known Manolo for long?" I asked on his return with the bottle and three glasses.

"It seems forever, but it is since our early twenties. He is two years older than me."

"Did you meet him through work?"

"In a way. We are both from the town, but we grew closer when we went to pick garlic together one spring, although it is not possible to get very close to Manolo."

"So have you worked together a lot over the years?"

"Ha, I see you wish to find out as much as you can about your enigmatic host before his return."

"Well, in a way, yes. He hasn't told me much about his past, or asked me about mine."

"No, and it is not likely that he will show much interest in your life, as he is a very egocentric person; kind and often generous, but egocentric. Yes, we have worked together on many occasions and we both shared one great disappointment."

"What was that?" I asked, hoping not to hear the sound of a car for a while yet.

"Well, you have probably realised from speaking to him and from our short conversation just now that we are both educated people, if that does not sound conceited."

"Yes. I mean, yes, you both seem educated, not conceited."

"Ha, well about twenty years ago we were both thoroughly fed up of working on the land, for other people, and we decided to study for an oposición together."

"What is an oposición?"

"They are state examinations which are held to select people for all public posts, from road sweepers to the highest civil servants. We studied for some administrative posts which we felt were well within our reach. Like many Spaniards, all we wished for was a safe job, a job for life, and we spent almost a year studying together almost every day."

"And what happened?"

"We both passed." Pepe held my gaze and paused for effect. "We both passed and we were both waiting to find out our destination, somewhere in the province of Cordoba, when we had our great disappointment." He sipped his beer and waited for me to speak, so I thought I'd better.

"What happened?"

"Well, they claimed that there had been some confusion over the marking of the examinations and the result was that we were pushed down the list of successful candidates; pushed off it, in fact. It was pure corruption of course. Somebody somewhere wanted different people to get the posts and they arranged it."

"Did you not complain?"

"Oh yes, about fifty of us went to Madrid to protest. Manolo had us all make placards and after our claims were rebuffed he suggested we go on hunger strike outside the government department building."

"Wow," I said, despite being fairly sure by then that Spanish people didn't say wow.

"Nobody else was prepared to go to such lengths, so he began the hunger strike alone. Two journalists came to speak to him and take photographs."

"How many days did he hold out for?"

"About eleven hours. In the evening while we were preparing to bed down for the night an old lady brought us large sandwiches wrapped in tinfoil. Manolo explained his intentions, so she gave them to me. I went around the corner to eat one and was about half done when Manolo appeared and held out his hand. I was struggling so hard to control my laughter that I was unable to open my mouth to convince him that he should resist the urge to eat, so he ate."

"Oh well, I don't suppose it would have worked anyway."

"But the story does not end there, Ken." Now he too appeared to be listening for an approaching car. "He continued the hunger strike for five more days."

Pepe had spoken very gravely so far, but I now saw that his suppressed mirth was getting the better of him.

"Go on," I said, eager to hear the outcome.

"Well, as I said, he continued the strike for five days, but only during the day. After nightfall I took him food – I was staying in a nearby hostel by this time – and he ate, rather like a Muslim during Ramadan. The same journalists came to see him every day, but became disappointed that he was not getting any thinner. On the sixth day they did not appear, so we came home." He gave me a broad smile for the first time and began to giggle. "It is the funniest thing that has happened to me in my whole life."

"Does Manolo see the funny side of it?"

"He does now, sometimes, but I would rather you didn't mention that I have told you."

"Of course not, but what was the point of pretending all that time?"

"Well, as they had cheated him, he saw no reason not to cheat them. If more interest had been generated I think he would have started to take it more seriously, but corruption of that kind is so common in this country that it did not make the news. That episode was the commencement of his radicalisation, I think. Although he later spent several years leading a normal life with Chelo, I think that the seed of rebellion had been planted."

"Chelo?"

"His girlfriend, who he almost married. It was after that ended that he bought this land and began to build his bunker."

"Chelo? Not Monica?"

"Monica came later, a very pretty girl. Yes, you see, at the time of the fictitious hunger strike he seemed to be wholly recovered from his first huge disappointment."

"What was that?" I asked, on the edge (cliché or not) of my seat. The sound of crunching gravel was followed by the application of squeaky brakes.

"When he gave up his studies in Madrid."

"What was he studying?" A car door opened and I heard footsteps.

"He was studying for the priesthood... Ah, Benítez, here you are at last!"

Not wishing to turn this story into theatre, I won't reproduce the ensuing conversation which I was too pensive to play much of a part in, but which consisted of a rather dull exchange between two friends who had either grown apart or had never been very close in the first place. On a later occasion Pepe told me that he had been afraid to engage me in any lengthy dialogues that evening lest a word or a phrase trigger off the hilarity that telling the hunger strike tale always remained within him for some time afterwards.

During the hour or so that he stayed, Manolo told him about what we had been up to and Pepe told him that although he hated work, not working for four months had made him even more depressed than working, but that a labouring job on an archaeological dig in the town was due to start the following week, which had cheered him up a bit and would at least not mean getting up at some ungodly hour to drive miles into the country. On this rather anticlimactic note and after being given a copy of El Sistema to read, he took his leave and promised to visit again soon.

"That's Pepe for you," said Manolo when we had moved inside and closed the door.

"Yes, he's not the happiest man I've ever met."

"Although I guess that you had a good chat before I arrived."

"Er, yes, we talked about this and that."

"Ha, he is a terrible gossip, I know, and I do not know how much one can count on him as a friend."

"Oh, I think you can count on him. That's the impression I got, anyway."

"Hmm, in some ways I would like him to come here to the project, but possibly at a later stage when we have begun to build houses on the land."

"He seems very attached to his mother though," I replied, based on some rather gloomy commentaries regarding her poor state of health.

"His mother is almost eighty, but is as strong as an ox. If he does not pull himself out of his cycles of depression she may even outlive him. Another day I will tell you about the time when we studied for an oposición together."

"Yes, do. I'd like to hear about that."

15

After the excitement of my first meeting with Pepe the only caller over the next couple of weeks was Eustacia, whose stews changed slightly due to her having opened a large bag of goats' meat from the freezer which she thought would make a nice change for the next few weeks. My cat reduction scheme had succeeded in getting their numbers down into single figures, but only just, whereupon she insisted that they be fed inside the compound, at least on the days of her visits.

"I come to see them too, as well as you and him," she said in the mock scolding voice that she now affected with both of us.

"How is your husband?"

"He seems all right, but I am concerned about his driving. His eyesight is not good, but he says that he has been driving up and down that road for so long that there is no danger. Don't tell Manolo about this or he will not allow him to drive me here," she said very seriously, which seemed odd, given her bossy manner with her son.

I was dying to delve more deeply into Manolo's priestly past and I was often alone with Eustacia during her visits, but I thought that it would be unethical to extract 'the goods' from his nearest and dearest, or even from Pepe, and decided to bide my time. The subject of religion was bound to come up sooner or later during our evening chats and my fast-improving Spanish would enable me to steer the conversation onto a more personal level.

We did plenty of work during those two weeks, so much, in fact, that I wondered what we would find to do during the winter months. One cloudy day we drove and rode out to the land to move the goats and plough the bottom field in preparation for the winter planting. There were two things I particularly wanted to learn how to do and it seemed the perfect opportunity to apprise Manolo of both of them.

"Oughtn't I to learn how to milk the goat, Manolo?" I asked as I stood watching him milk her.

"Yes, I suppose you could, but it is not as easy as it looks," he said as the milk spurted into the pan. "I have started now, but another day you can try."

"Vale."

"But it is not easy. Not everyone can do it."

"I'd like to learn. By the way, I think that the other he-goat is strong enough to come to join the others now," I said, flaunting my animal-healing credentials. "He is eating well and has gained weight."

"Good, yes, we will bring him in the trailer soon and see if he is now capable of doing the job that I bought him for. How is the mare doing now?" he asked, having scarcely passed the time of day with her for several weeks.

"Well, she is eating better, especially when I take her down to the river, and her coat is a bit shinier, and she seems happy enough, but she seems no more inclined to trot than before," I said, still feeling embarrassed enough about riding her down the road bareback to wish to get that part of the journey over with more quickly.

"Hmm, she has never done much trotting, even when I first bought her and she was full of health. Trotting is not very comfortable without a saddle, you know."

"No, I suppose not. I could buy one for her."

"Uf, a saddle is a very expensive item."

"Second hand?"

"Still very expensive for such an old horse." His eyes brightened. "But, we could make one for her."

"Make one?"

"Yes, I once intended to make a harness for her, and build a little cart too, so a saddle would be easy in comparison." He poured the goat's milk into a screw-top bottle. "Now I must plough the land," he said, setting off towards the tractor.

"That is something else I'd quite like to learn how to do, drive the tractor."

"Uf, this tractor is a very dangerous old machine. It is not stable like the newer ones and is especially lethal on a sloping field. A man near Écija was killed a few years ago when his tractor, similar to this one, fell on top of him."

"But this part of the land is almost flat."

"Yes, but it is also difficult to start and to drive. Tomorrow I will show you how to milk the goat."

"Right," I said, somewhat bemused by his logic, "I'll head off back to the house then."

Sensing my annoyance, he smiled and pushed back his hair.

"The tractor is not insured, you see. That is why I leave it on the land and drive it to the house only rarely. I brought it up from town on a truck when the other project ended, which was very expensive." He winced at the thought. "And if anything happened to the animal expert, what would happen to the project?"

"Hmm."

"Anyway, in a couple of years I intend to be ploughing the land with horses, or even oxen if I can get hold of them, so your role will be of increasing importance."

'Fat chance of me being stuck here in the back of beyond two years from now,' I thought. "Vale," I said, before watching him plough a couple of furrows on the seemingly stable tractor that had started first time.

As Yegua and I plodded back to the house, I decided to give Manolo the benefit of the doubt over his reticence regarding the tractor. Perhaps he was concerned for my safety, after all, and was not just set on confining me to doing all the tasks that he found least agreeable, as I had first surmised. By this time, you see, although I still couldn't imagine my stay at El Refugio lasting far beyond Christmas, I was becoming enthusiastic about this farming business and was eager to learn all I could about it, including tractor driving and goat milking, before I moved on to pastures new, possibly even literally, as I was sure that there must be more serious agricultural projects established in other parts of Spain which would welcome more seasoned recruits. Time will tell, I thought, and left it at that.

Never one to dally once he had got the figurative bit between his teeth, Manolo suggested that we begin the winter planting that same afternoon. After ribbing him briefly about the crops being his department – just to keep him aware of my lingering discontent – we filled the boot of his battered old car with bags of the no less decrepit potatoes, onions and (slightly better preserved) garlic bulbs that we had shifted out of the storeroom, chucked in a couple of azadas, and headed off to the land.

As with the beans in the upper field, Manolo wasn't one to mess around measuring distances and depths, so long before nightfall we had put the remnants of last winter's underground crops back where they had come from, having this time taken turns at scooping out the earth and popping in the spuds, onions and garlic cloves.

"There, that is done," said Manolo, hardly tired at all by our three hours' speedy work.

"Shouldn't we water it all?" I asked while I pummelled some life into my lower back.

"Yes, but it can wait until tomorrow."

"It might rain," I said, looking at the clear sky.

"I doubt it, but even if it did, we must lay the irrigation tubes as we will have to water at some point. It will rain hard soon, but during the winter there will be dry periods, I am sure."

After breakfast the next day, Yegua and I enjoyed a sunny stroll out to the land, where Manolo was already lugging the petrol motor from the car to the stream.

"I can't remember where anything is," I said as I surveyed the field.

"Oh, it doesn't matter. We will know when the plants sprout. Winter crops are never very abundant, but with our sunny weather and excellent soil it would be a crime not to make the most of it."

Once we had stretched the tubes out along each furrow, we connected them to the main pipe and after I had made half a dozen unsuccessful attempts to pull-start the motor, practicing my Spanish oaths as I did so, Manolo's first deft yank got it going.

Aware of my frustration and perhaps fearing a repeat of yesterday's sulks, he spoke.

"Don't worry. The motor, like the tractor, will soon be a thing of the past. When we have built the water deposit up there, and if the gods are kind enough to give us rain, we will begin to dispense with all mechanised aids."

('Gods?' Had he turned polytheist or pagan since chucking his church studies? I *had* to find out soon.)

"Let us go to see if the beans have sprouted while this is being watered," he concluded.

The panorama of patchy greenery which greeted us as we crested the rise was not of the kind to delight the eye, as there were far more weeds than visible bean sprouts.

"Hmm, as I thought," he said. "The little rain we have had has encouraged all growth. Ha, if we had brought the azadas, we could have cleaned it up in no time."

I was almost certain that those instruments of torture were still in the back of the car, but didn't say so. Instead I asked if him it was time for me to milk the goat.

"Ah, yes, it is time, but I forgot to bring the pan and the bottle. No matter, you can have a go at milking her without the pan."

"Isn't that a waste?" I asked, not that I had developed a taste for the stuff yet; I still preferred the bovine variety that Eustacia brought from the supermarket.

"I have plenty of milk just now and you will have enough to think about learning to manipulate the teats without also worrying about where it is going." We approached the goat. "Even so, you must pretend that there is a pan on the ground or the next time you try you will be no nearer to catching the milk. Now, crouch down to her left. Good, now, you must not pull, you must trap the milk between your finger and thumb and then use the other fingers to squeeze the milk out. Hmm, the action is correct but no milk is coming out. Let me show you."

"No, no, I must do it myself," I said, fighting to keep the restless beast in position over the hypothetical pan. On my third or fourth attempt a few drops of milk dribbled out and just when the goat appeared to be about to try to bolt away from her tormentor, the first real spurt drained into the ground and she relaxed.

"Very good. Now try to milk the other teat with your other hand."

Left-handed milking, however, proved to be beyond me and I remained a unidextrous milker for the several days that it took me to get all of the milk into the receptacle. (The only downside of the milking chore which I carried out almost every day from then on was that most of my horse rides were thenceforth to the land, rather than down to the luxuriant riverbank where my steed always ate her fill, but more about mare-matters later.)

That same afternoon Manolo suggested that we pop back to the land to clear those few weeds from the bean field, which would take us two ticks, before nipping back home well before sunset. That is not, of course, anywhere near a literal translation of what he actually said, but when we arrived at the field via the higher track I soon saw that his intimation that it would be a quick job was euphemistic to say the least. By the time I slumped down into the passenger seat, shortly *after* sunset, we had succeeded in covering about half of the furrows and my thirst was far greater than even that of the half-abandoned beans.

"Yes, we should have brought some water to drink," said my fresh-faced companion. "I too am a little thirsty now. Tomorrow we will soon finish the weeding and then we can water the beans again."

The reader may have noticed – I certainly had – that Manolo had by now replaced his former 'I' with 'we' when referring to the execution of the next jobs on the agenda and I almost told him that the next day I intended to go for a (very undemanding) bike ride. Peer pressure is a powerful thing, however, and I consoled myself with the thought that once the autumn rains came there would be little for us to do on the land. The next day's weeding (a.m.) and bucket hauling (p.m.) left me feeling quite worn out, but the fact that I was not a solid mass of aches and pains the following day indicated that I was becoming accustomed to this type of toil.

That day, a Saturday, saw the long awaited return of Lola, whose inimitable hand-braking was followed by a loud rap on the gate.

"She knows it is open," Manolo said to me as we sat drinking our coffee on the terrace, "but she likes to make a noise. Come in, Lola, it is open!"

"How did you know it was me?" she asked as she walked down the drive closely followed by a dark, thin, teenage boy carrying a plastic bag containing her usual liquid offerings.

"We just knew," said Manolo.

"Mohammed, meet Manolo and Ken."

"Buenas tardes, I am pleased to meet you both," said the handsome young lad in what seemed to me to be a perfect Spanish accent.

"Do you like the countryside?" I asked him after we had both shook his hand.

"I don't know it very well, not this kind of countryside, anyway."

"Mohammed was brought up in the refugee camp in Algeria where the evil Moroccan government forced them to go to once they had expelled them from their own country. He has only been in Spain for a few months," Lola explained.

"Your Spanish is very good," I said to the boy. "Much better than mine."

"I am…"

"The Sahrawies study Spanish as their second language," interrupted Lola, "as they have done ever since they were part of the evil Spanish empire."

"How do you like school here?" I asked quickly, determined to let him speak for himself.

"Oh, it is all right, but hard for me."

"He struggles in class because his writing is not so good, and-"

"In two years I will be sixteen," Mohammed said, cutting Lola off quite assertively. "Then I will be able to work and earn money for my family."

"But you must study," she said.

"While I have to," he said.

"You must study a lot and get qualifications," she said.

"What for?" he asked. "We always do the worst jobs anyway."

"Not if you study, at least until you are eighteen," she said.

"Ha! I will be working before then, if we have not taken up arms against the Moroccans and I have returned to fight."

"The only weapon you will be taking up is your pen," she said, "and I am sure that Ken or Manolo will help you with your homework while I just pop into town to pick up next week's sewing."

This carefully reconstructed conversation is indicative of two things: the argumentative relationship which had already been established between Lola and her ward and that spirited woman's resolve to allow us to share the burden of his education. Before any of us could speak she was marching back up the drive after promising to be back within an hour or two.

They say that good writers show rather than tell, so I'll let the reader make his or her mind up about what the following conversation infers.

"So, Mohammed," I began. "How is life with Lola so far?"

"Uf, she is a kind lady, but can be very bossy and we argue a lot. In my family the women don't normally argue so much."

"I suppose it's for your own good, though," I said. "Don't you think so, Manolo?"

"Er, yes," he said after removing the pipe from his mouth. "Are you interested in agriculture?" he asked the boy.

"I don't really know much about it."

"How would you like to help me collect the last tomatoes over there and then pull up the plants?"

"I'd like to, but if I don't do my homework she will be angry,"

Vale, I will begin and when you and Ken have finished the homework you will find me over beyond the stable."

So it was that the barely literate (in Spanish) Englishman pulled his chair closer to that of the unenthusiastic scholar who had begun to fish a plethora of textbooks out of his orange rucksack, while Manolo sidled away to the sanctuary of his tomato plantation.

I suggested that we start with Maths, reasoning that numbers were the same in any language, and although the Spanish method of doing long division was quite different to how I remembered it, we were able to dispatch the dozen or so questions within about half an hour. We then moved onto History and between the two of us we managed to compose a few apposite sentences regarding the Spanish-American War of 1898, an event that I vaguely remembered touching upon in one of my university courses. By the time we had begun to tackle the Spanish Language homework both of us were getting rather restless, Mohammed through boredom and me through a desire to hear the crunch of Lola's handbrake or the emergence of Manolo from the tomato plot due to my ignorance of Spanish grammatical terms.

Manolo was the first to come to my aid and after passing his soiled finger over the page and pointing out the correct answers – which was hardly cricket – he returned to his duties and left me to help my almost comatose student with his English exercises, allowing me at least to finish on a high note. As soon as Mohammed had thanked me, bundled away his books and rushed off to help Manolo rip out the remaining plants, Lola returned with exquisite timing and bewailed the fact that we had not even started to do the homework.

"We have finished the homework, just a moment ago, in fact," I said primly, wishing we had had the foresight to leave the books on the table.

"Oh, thank goodness. Who helped him?"

"Me, mostly."

"Ah, you are a saint. I left school at fifteen, you see, to join the student protests in Madrid, and I don't want to lose Mohammed's respect by showing him how uneducated I am. It is good to know that another person with solidarity will help him each week."

"Er, but I still struggle with Spanish myself."

"Yes, but two heads are better than one. Would you like a beer?"

Thus bribed into acquiescence, I had polished off two glasses by the time the two toilers had piled up all the old plants and returned to the terrace.

"Work is better than study," said a beaming Mohammed, his burst of activity having erased his previous lethargy. "What else is there to do, Manolo?"

"I don't know. Ken looks after the animals now."

"You could go to see if there are any eggs, I suppose," I said.

"Where are they?"

"Oh, they could be anywhere within their fences. Take an egg box from the kitchen top and see if you can fill it," I said, keen to see what my friend would have to say in his absence.

After Mohammed had sprinted off down the slope, Manolo put down his glass of water and looked at Lola.

"So, Lola, what is your idea regarding Mohammed coming here?" he asked with a grave look.

"Well, I think it will be good for him to come to the country and learn a few things."

"What kind of things?" he asked.

"Well, about the animals and the plants, and a little more about his school subjects."

"What do you think about that, Ken?" he asked, turning his solemn gaze upon me.

"Well, I don't mind helping him out as much as I'm able, but I'm not exactly the best person for the job. I struggled today and I have a feeling that it was quite easy stuff."

"I am sure Manolo will help with the more difficult things," said Lola with a winning smile.

"No, I won't," he said. "When he comes he can help me on the land and I will teach him things that will be useful. If Ken wishes to try to tutor him is his concern, but I have no desire to perform that task. How often do you intend to bring him, Lola?"

"On Saturdays, and I thought that he might stay over until Sunday sometimes."

"No, Ken and I want peace and quiet in the evenings. We read and sometimes chat and hardly ever watch television."

My face expressed, I think, neither agreement nor discrepancy with Manolo's assertion as I awaited Lola's reaction.

"Vale, well, we will be going now," she said in a rather wounded voice. "Thank you for helping him with his homework, Ken, and I will see you both soon. Mohammed! We must go now!" she shouted down the land.

I accompanied an effusive Mohammed and a very tight-lipped Lola to the gate and said goodbye from there before returning to the terrace.

"Weren't you a little hard on her?" I asked my complacent-looking companion.

"For how long have you known Lola?"

"Well, you know how long."

"I have known her for many years. One must be firm with her. I swear that if I had not made myself so clear, a month from now she would be dropping him off on Friday afternoons and collecting him on Sunday evenings. She assumes too much of people."

"He seems like a nice lad, though."

"Yes, he does, and if Lola were not as she is, he could spend more time here, but I know that she would soon make us feel that we were also responsible for his upbringing."

"Do you think so?"

"I know it. He would spend all the school holidays here."

"Surely not."

"We would have to buy him clothes and books. Who knows, if she took up with another of her stupid boyfriends, he might end up *living* here."

"Does she often take up with... boyfriends?"

"She was married once, in fact she has two grown daughters, but after that she became very liberal in her relations, and very poor at choosing her partners. Two or three have passed by here, but I did not make them very welcome. She disregards her political beliefs when she takes a fancy to one sex-starved imbecile or another."

"Well, I don't know her very well," I said, pouring the dregs from the beer bottle into my glass.

"I seemed harsh but, as I say, I know her. I also think that you will find it quite challenging enough to fulfil your weekly tutoring duties," he said before emitting the first laugh that had been heard for some time.

"But do you think she'll even come next week? She looked very upset."

"Ha, ha, next week we will hear the handbrake and her calls from the track and she will enter as if nothing has happened. She is very thick-skinned."

"I hope so, I mean, I hope they come."

"They will come. Do not worry about that."

16

Manolo confessed the next day that one reason why he had been so abrupt with Lola was that she had not so much as mentioned his book.

"She makes demands of us, but has clearly not been willing to spend just three or four hours reading my book," he said while I watched him repairing a contraption called a mula mecánica.

"I should finish it very soon and will tell you what I think then," I said, though I had finished it days ago and was still trying to decide how critical my feedback ought to be.

"Thank you. None of the Sevillians have contacted me about it yet, but after their visit I am not so sure that they are very serious people after all. There, now it should start. Would you like to have a go at ploughing the area where the tomatoes were?"

He started the manual plough – rather like an oversize petrol lawnmower, but with very sharp teeth – and twisted the throttle gently to allow him to propel it over the gravel to the land in question. Once in position he increased the revs, upon which the rotating blades dug in deeply and churned up the earth most effectively as they pulled the noisy machine along. After completing two narrow rows he explained the controls to me and stood aside.

Manolo had made it look like the machine was doing all the work, but I had to exert great force just to keep it on the straight and narrow, while turning it round at the end of the row required even more effort. By the time I had ploughed the small area under my mentor's watchful eye, my arms and shoulders felt like I had been wrestling with a small bear, or how I imagine that feels.

"That is harder than it looks," I said, mopping my brow.

"Well, it didn't look easy, the way you were straining this way and that, ha, ha. It gets easier with practice. Perhaps we could plant some more potatoes on the strips of land down there between the fruit trees."

"Do we need more potatoes? I mean, we planted a lot in the field."

"Hmm, perhaps we don't, but who knows how many people will be here in the spring."

'About one,' I thought.

"I forgot to ask Pepe if he placed the advertisement," he went on. "I expected to receive some calls by now. I will ring him."

When he had disappeared into the house I performed my animal feeding chores, found a few eggs, and reminded myself that it was time to clean out the pigsty again.

"He says that he did place the advertisement, but that he will update it one day soon. Hmm, I wonder if he did," he said when I had returned to the terrace.

"I'm sure he did."

"Yes, I think so, but I am surprised that nobody has called."

"Perhaps the next time Pepe comes up we could sit down together and compose a new advert?"

"Yes, I might have worded the first one in too serious a manner. Maybe we should dispense with the socio-political reasons for coming to El Refugio and just make it sound like a little working holiday."

"I think that would be best. Did Pepe say when he was going to come?"

"Ha, until he finishes work on the archaeological dig I doubt that we will see him. He reacts very badly to physical work and was just complaining how he can hardly move in the evenings due to fatigue. He says the job will end in a week or two, so we will see him after that. I hope he has read my book by then."

Thus it was that after Lola and Mohammed's visit we, or rather I, suffered another lengthy period of isolation, apart from Eustacia's stew-making and housekeeping expeditions, as the end of the summer crops saw the end of Luisa for a while and Manolo was proven wrong about Lola not holding his harsh words against him.

"She is either sulking or has found another tutor," he said one day when we had attached the trailer to the car and transported the old billy goat to join the rest of the 'herd' on the land. He looked up at the cloudy sky. "Hmm, I think there will be heavy rain later."

"We've seen a lot of clouds lately, but hardly any rain," I said, watching the goat renewing his acquaintance with the others.

"It will soon be November. Yes, there will be heavy rain and then the temperature will fall."

I had already noticed a certain chilliness when getting up in the mornings and Manolo had begun to light wood fires in the chimney of an evening, as much for their soothing effect as for any real need for them, but after the downpour that did indeed take place that night and all the following day, the weather became distinctly cooler.

"Where do you keep the firewood?" I asked him on the evening after the rain had begun.

"There, you can see it," he said, pointing to the small pile beside the fire.

"Is that all?"

"There is a little more round the side of the house, but we will need to get some when the rain stops."

"Do you buy it?"

"Ha, of course not. Nature provides us with all the firewood we need. You know the woods by the river where you sometimes take the mare? There is our supply."

"Is that allowed?" asked the veteran of forty-nine years of obedience to almost all British laws.

"I don't see why not. Luckily, very few people are industrious enough to find their own firewood these days. Tomorrow it will be fine again and we will make a little trip."

The 'little trip' proved to be an exhausting morning-long expedition spent foraging for dead, or nearly dead, pine branches in the steep woodland beside the river. Breaking off huge branches and stepping aside as they fell to the ground was easy enough, but the fact that most of them were a long way down the slope from where the car and trailer were parked appeared to be an almost insurmountable obstacle.

"Won't we have to bring the chainsaw and chop these up?" I asked, eying a ten foot long branch which must have weighed as much as me.

"No, we don't want to attract too much attention. We will drag them up."

So we dragged and heaved and sweated and cursed until the last of the branches were in the trailer and hanging over the top of the car in a very unstable way. Manolo tied a few together and we headed for our respective car doors.

"Er. Ken, I think it will be better if you walk alongside the car. It is not far and you can bang on the roof if you see that one is about to fall off."

Despite it not being far and although I was becoming immune to ridicule after so many bareback rides along the road, I did not enjoy our absurd procession past the petrol station and was relieved that the Civil Guard jeep was not parked outside as it sometimes was while the olive-clad policemen refreshed themselves within. After dragging all the branches out onto the area in front of the house, Manolo, instead of suggesting a rest like any normal person, brought the chainsaw from the garage and was about to fire it up.

"Should we not wait until after lunch?" I asked.

"It is only one o'clock. I will just spend half an hour cutting, to work up an appetite."

"I'll go to milk the goat then," I said, not in the mood to listen to the noisy saw in my fatigued state.

"Vale. Oh, it will be a little muddy after the rain. I would tie the mare to one of the neighbour's trees and walk across his land to the goats. You will need your boots."

"Will it be so bad?"

"You will see."

If I ever thought of mud in the past it was of churned up football fields, but the horrendously squelchy, sticky substance into which I sank after stepping onto the neighbour's field was more reminiscent of First World War literature than anything I had ever experienced. With each step I sank up to a foot into the earth and on dragging out my boot I found a heavy mass of mud firmly attached to it. By the time I had reached the disconsolate-looking goats I was ready to sit down, but as there was nowhere to sit I sank myself into position and milked the beast, who was less fidgety than usual with her hooves stuck in the ground.

On my return, Manolo laid down the saw and watched me clean my boots with a stick.

"Yes, very muddy, as I thought," he said, smiling sympathetically.

"Yes, it was hard work to get to them," I replied, almost wishing I had never insisted on learning how to milk in the first place. "I think the goats will need a bigger and better place to shelter. They didn't look very happy out there in the mud and the old male was hogging the pallet hut, which is pretty useless anyway."

"They are very hardy animals."

"Yes, but I doubt that much breeding will go on in those conditions."

"Don't worry, I have a plan to build a pen on the land with little shelters for when the weather gets really cold."

"Oh?"

"Yes, a moveable pen of my own design, so that they can be transferred from one part of the land to another in order to keep the weeds down. We will wait for the land to dry before we begin."

After two more muddy milking days, during which time I also cleaned the pigsty and managed to get out on one of my increasingly rare bike rides, the land was deemed fit enough to begin the construction of the goat pen.

The tools and materials we took to the land with which to construct this still undisclosed structure consisted of a hammer and many long nails, an electric screwdriver and many long screws, a large coil of thick twine and a pocket knife.

"What are we going to build it out of?" I asked as he brought the car to a halt next to the bean field.

"Those pallets over there," he replied, pointing to several piles of them lined up just over the border with the neighbouring land.

"Are they yours?"

"They are now. I called the owner of the land and he says I can have them. He had forgotten about them, so rarely does he come to look at his olive trees now that his son has taken over the work."

"Might the son not want them for something?"

"Too late, in a few hours they will form part of a permanent structure."

"I thought it was going to be movable?"

"That too. Come on."

Perplexed, I followed him down the still sticky earth track to the piles of pallets, from where he surveyed his domain.

"Yes, half way down the slope where the fruit trees will be is the best spot. The first thing we have to do is carry them down there."

Carrying one slimy, rain-sodden pallet about a hundred yards down sticky land is no great feat, but carrying about twenty of them (each) is a very tiresome and tiring process, at the end of which I sat down on one to recover.

"This is the plan," said Manolo, still standing. "First we will construct four shelters for the goats using four pallets for each, like the one down there."

"I get the idea. Won't they leak a bit?"

"Ha, ha, I like your English humour. Later we will cover at least the top one with plastic."

"And there are five goats."

"Yes, but I am sure that two of them will not mind sharing. So, we build the shelters and place them in a square formation before joining them together with more pallets, one of which will be a gate for us to enter."

"Vale, but how is that movable?"

"Well, and this is the brilliant part of my idea, when they have eaten all the grass and weeds from the first area, we simply turn the circle around onto the adjacent bit of land. That way, when the time comes to plant the trees, the whole slope should be relatively free of weeds. That is called efficient, ecological farming."

"Won't the shelters be facing the wrong way if we pull the sides round to make another circle?"

"Hmm, perhaps, but in any case it will be easy to move. Let us begin."

After placing the pallets roughly where we wanted them, we propped up the first shelter and Manolo began to nail it together, before inserting a few token screws to give the construction more credibility.

"There," he said, "they will be much cosier with one of those to themselves."

"If we cover them with plastic."

"Yes. I think it will be easier if we first form the circle of pallets and then incorporate the shelters, don't you think?"

Surprised at being asked, I said I supposed so, and we spent the rest of the morning lashing pallets together with the strong twine.

"Good, now we just have to come back to build the remaining shelters after lunch."

When we returned after lunch the circle had collapsed, so we propped it back up before building a second shelter opposite to the first one, after which the higher of the two semi-circles collapsed.

"Don't you think it would be better to build five or, better still, six shelters to make the structure more solid?" I asked him.

"Hmm, perhaps, but we don't have enough pallets."

"There's the other shelter down there where the goats are."

"Oh, we will leave that for... for something else. Four will be fine."

Overruled, but confident that I was storing up an 'I told you so' for future use, I helped him to build the last two shelters, after which we surveyed our rather unsightly handiwork.

"I think it could do with a bit more reinforcement," I felt obliged to say. "I mean, if it gets windy it might fall down."

"The winds are rarely very strong in this area and it is more solid than it looks."

"Vale."

"Let us fetch the goats."

After leading them up the land and releasing them into their new home, we closed the pallet gate and observed them as they tucked in to the freshest weeds.

"It won't take them long to clean all this up," I said. "We'll have to move it all soon."

"Hmm, we can bring them hay and we (meaning you) can always bring them some more weeds from around here. A job well done, I think."

"When we've covered the shelters with plastic."

"You are very concerned for the comfort of the beasts, ha, ha. Tomorrow we will do that and also bring them a large water receptacle, *and*," he added, striving to please, "when it rains again it won't be quite so difficult to reach the goat to milk it. Goodnight, goats!" he cried, in excellent spirits as he always was after a back-breaking day's work.

The next morning we returned in the car with a large water container, an old capazo to use as a bowl, a small bale of hay and all the plastic sheets and sacks that we had been able to find. One quarter of the goat pen was leaning inwards and the goats had gone. One look at Manolo's furious countenance told me not to tell him I had told him so, so I just waited for his reaction.

"I shit myself on the whore mother!" he said, the worst expletive I had ever heard him say, and one of the worst which the language possesses. "Those damn animals will be eating the leaves of the olive trees. I hope they are on my sister's land and not on the other side."

"What shall we do?"

"Find them, of course," he snapped.

"I mean, do we go together, or do we split up."

"Yes, you look on my sister's land and I will look on the neighbour's. Approach them slowly. It is lucky that I left a short rope around their necks," he said, before sprinting away like a Red Indian out to do a spot of scalping.

I trotted over to his sister's olive trees and saw the milkable goat, another she-goat and the old male who we had brought from the house, all tucking into the leaves of the trees at the far end of the field. As I walked slowly towards them, I saw that they had already attended to the lower branches of all the trees on either side of me, but hadn't done much real damage. Hearing some furious cursing from the other field made me more determined than ever to adopt a softly-softly approach to the task in hand and I reasoned that my intimacy with the one I milked might make her the easiest to catch.

When I got within twenty yards of them I stopped to observe their reaction to my arrival, which was similar to that of teenagers being collected from a party, not really wanting to go home, but realising that it was late and there was no point arguing. I sauntered towards my quarry, whistling nonchalantly, and managed to put my foot on the rope just before she moved away. After patting her gratefully on the head, I led her slowly towards the other she-goat and trapped her rope easily enough. As the geriatric male was looking at me suspiciously, and having my hands quite full, I walked the pretty young things past him and just hoped that what little remained of his macho instincts would induce him to follow us. By walking very slowly back towards their pen and not denying them a last few nibbles, I succeeded in coaxing the aged one along with us and after tying the other two to a pallet, I presented him with a large, juicy weed and grabbed his rope.

I saw that another young goat was tied to a pallet on the far side of the pen, but the sound of furious shrieks and bellows from among the neighbour's tree told me that two old males were still on the loose, one chasing after the other. Modesty forbids me from comparing and contrasting my goat capturing method with that of their owner's, but I must say that I had never before seen a fifty-two-year-old man make a series of such rapid sprints, only to be outpaced every time by the olive leaf-fuelled veteran whose agility also surprised me.

By the time I had trotted round to head off the goat, however, Manolo had finally captured him and was teaching him the error of his ways by banging his fist down on his head with all his might and calling him all sorts of names. When he saw me approach, he cut short the corporal punishment and handed me the rope.

"Take him, Ken, or I swear that I will beat him to death," he said, still panting from his exertions and rubbing his hand. "And the others?"

"Tied up," I said, before turning away and leading the hard-headed beast, who seemed none the worse for wear, back to the pen.

When Manolo joined me a few minutes later he was contrite.

"Goats have very hard heads, you know," he said, not quite looking at me. "And I had to show him that he had done wrong."

"I'm not sure goats are clever enough to know the difference between right and wrong," I said, stroking the old goat's head.

"How did you catch those three?" he asked, so I explained my method.

"Yes, you have a way with animals that I do not possess."

"Listen, Manolo, if I see you doing anything like that again, I'll have to leave."

"Right, yes, you are right, it does no good. The next time they escape I will let you take the lead, *but*," his tone becoming sanguine more quickly than I would have liked, "if we use the four pallets down by the river as supports for each quarter of the circle, it will not collapse again."

"Hmm."

"If I go back to get the tools and you begin to… no, better still, if you go back to get the tools and I bring up the pallets, we can reinforce the structure in no time."

"That means me driving the car."

"Here are the keys."

"Is it insured for me?"

"I think so. I will check later. I should find out anyway as one day you may wish to drive down into town," he said, dangling the peace-offering from his fingers.

'Give me the tractor keys too and I'll forgive you,' I thought as I suppressed my urge to laugh at his schoolboy ways.

I took the keys and drove the car, which handled better than it looked, back to the house for the tools. When I returned, Manolo had dragged the four pallet shelter up the slope to the pen, a tremendous feat of strength for any man, let alone a middle-aged one who had just spent half an hour chasing a goat. After dismantling the shelter we nailed and screwed the pallets at right angles to each quarter of the circle – the higher two on the inside and the lower two on the outside – after which it looked much more stable.

"A job well done," he said, collecting the tools.

"We still have to put the plastic sheets on."

"Ah, yes, let us do it now."

After watching him hurriedly cutting into a plastic sheet without taking measurements, I asked him to wait a moment.

"These nails are far too long. I don't think any rain is forecast, so why don't I cover the shelters little by little when I come to milk the goat and give them food and water?" I said after quickly deciding that longer trips to the land would get me away from the house and out of some of the little jobs that he was constantly dreaming up.

"Yes, of course, if you want. Goodbye, goats," said the penitent in his most animal-friendly voice. "Ken will come to see you soon."

17

The few days before Pepe's next visit were curious ones. While I busied myself with the animals and riding Yegua out to the land to leisurely cover the goat shelters with plastic, Manolo didn't seem to be doing very much at all, apart from reading and working on the manuscript which I knew I would have to provide a critique of very soon. He seemed quite withdrawn, though always polite to me, and I was perfectly happy to let this state of affairs go on, if not indefinitely, certainly for a week or two more.

As my workload was not high and I managed to get out on my bike a couple of times, I didn't resent the fact that he was not pulling his weight in the least. I was enjoying my daily routine and learning more about animal behaviour and after almost two months at El Refugio I had still spent less than €100, effectively buying myself two more months on the road whenever I chose to move on. At this rate, I thought, I would reach the end of my sabbatical almost as economically secure as when I began it and would have the whole summer to find somewhere to settle down. Although I had promised to stay on until Christmas, and was quite happy to do so, I had already decided that I ought to set myself new challenges for the new year and that it was very unlikely that these new goals would be achievable in my current environment.

After these tranquil days it was, nevertheless, a great pleasure to open the gate to Pepe one dark evening and usher him into the warm living room.

"Ah, it is good to see an open fire," he said after placing his cold litre of beer on the table. "How are you, Benítez?" he asked the bespectacled scholar who replaced his bookmark and half stood to shake Pepe's hand.

"Not bad, Pepe. I am just reading an economics book to refresh my memory on the subject of price elasticity. I suppose you will be reading a lot again now that you have finished work on the excavation," he said, steering the conversation with an impressive lack of subtlety onto the subject that he was determined to discuss.

"Ah, the excavation! Thank goodness it is over. All that digging and brushing quite wore me out."

"What were you excavating, and who for?" I asked.

"Two archaeologists from Seville University came to do a little digging next to one of the churches, looking for Roman remains."

"Did you find any?"

"A little pottery, nothing more. Écija is a very historical town, but to excavate properly one would have to tear down some buildings and go down deeper and over a larger area. Before the Romans there was an Iberian settlement there. Would you like a glass of beer?" he asked us both.

After I had consented and Manolo had opted for a glass of water, I saw no point in putting off the inevitable.

"I finished your book, by the way," I said to Manolo, glancing at Pepe for support.

"I too have read it," said Pepe, before sipping his beer and falling silent.

"And what do you think of it? Manolo asked me.

"Well, I enjoyed it," I fibbed, "although it is still quite difficult for me to read in Spanish," which was true enough in this case.

"Yes?"

"Well, the first part all seems to make sense, about where we are going wrong as a society, I mean, and the second part is interesting, but very radical."

"That is the idea," Manolo said with a chuckle, his eyes urging me to go on.

"Radical and impractical," Pepe interjected, much to my relief. "The idea of dispensing with electricity and gas in a European country is absurd and unnecessary. The idea of a separate agricultural community is good in itself, if you can persuade enough people to buy land in one area to make it viable. The problem is that the people who have the means to buy large areas of land are not the kind of people who would be interested in such a scheme."

"I see your point," said Manolo, pushing himself up into debating position, "but these things start in a small way. If my sister agreed to join and we later added our parents' land, it could form the nucleus of an ever-expanding circle. You, for example, might then buy some adjacent fields, or Ken might do so, and as more people join the project, more land is bought."

"I don't know about Ken, but I have less money than a toothless prostitute, and the type of people who would be likely to come here probably won't have any either."

"You never know," I said, keen to inject a touch of optimism into the proceedings. "Were we not going to write a new advertisement for the project?"

"So, neither of you thinks that my book will inspire people to change?" asked the author.

"No, because people are too conservative, or stupid, or both of those things to desire any change that does not involve acquiring more possessions," said Pepe.

"Oh, I don't know," I said. "I think some people want change. I'm not saying that Spain is more backwards…"

"It is," said Pepe.

"But in Britain and other countries in northern Europe, there are more and more people getting interested in alternative lifestyles, even people with money."

"There must be some suitable people here in Spain, too," said Manolo.

"Yes, let's write that advert and see if we can find them," I said.

"Very well," he said, "but I would like us (meaning me and him) to discuss my book in more detail sometime. Pepe is too entrenched in modern society to appreciate my idea, although it seems to me that modern society has failed him just as it has failed so many people."

I thought that if Pepe could manage more than a few weeks work at a time, modern society might treat him more generously, but I decided to save that subject for when he and I were alone together.

"I'll get some paper," I said, "and you can give me some ideas."

In the event, Manolo's ideas were too politicised and Pepe's too discouraging, so the new advert was mostly my own work. It read something like this:

EL REFUGIO: Small, friendly agricultural project in southern Spain, currently home to two permanent residents as well as several local collaborators, welcomes visits from people of all ages and nationalities who are interested in sustainable agriculture and communal living. Food and living accommodation is provided and visitors will be encouraged to take part in all activities. For more information, please telephone Manolo Benítez on: ...

All this in Spanish, of course, but as an afterthought I suggested to Pepe that he post it in English too. On completing our first draft, Manolo snatched it up and took it to the computer to type it up, after which I added an English version.

"If you had the internet, you could email it to me," said Pepe, "although if you had the internet you could do it yourselves."

"Where are you going to put it?" I asked.

"Oh, I will do a search for suitable sites and forums and post it there."

"How much will it cost?" asked Manolo. "And how much do I owe you for the first one?"

"Ha, nothing at all. It is not an advertisement as such. The internet is a community in which one can participate freely, and for free. You should install it, but of course you cannot access it without electricity."

"Ha, we will have that for a while yet, but the internet is still a mystery to me," said Manolo. "Thank you for your help, Pepe. I am sure this advertisement will work."

"They will be queuing up at the gates. Did Lola come with Mohammed, by the way?"

"She came, she saw, she asked too much, and she left, ha, ha," said Manolo.

"She will return," said Pepe.

"That is what I told Ken."

Most of the month of November slipped by pleasantly enough without any major upsets or excitement, partly because Manolo, still in his studious mode, did nothing to rock the boat. The pigs were now fattening apace and it was a bitter-sweet experience to feed them and tease them while cleaning their sty because the fatter they got, the sooner they would meet their demise. One cool morning I discovered that one of the younger goats had escaped from the pallet pen and as she didn't prove quite so easy to extract from amid the olive trees as the last time, I decided to tell Manolo about it.

"Hmm," he said, laying aside his history book, "I feared that this would happen and now that they realise it can be done, it will occur more often. After lunch we will remedy the situation."

Over coffee we came to the conclusion that stringing a wire about a foot above the height of the pallets should be enough to dissuade any more bids for freedom.

"I think I have a roll of barbed wire in the garage," he said.

"Er, I would prefer not to use that, if you don't mind."

"No, of course not," he said quickly, perhaps still conscious of his tarnished animal rights reputation. "Normal wire will be perfectly adequate."

In the three hours of sunlight that remained, we hammered some posts onto the pallets between the now almost waterproof shelters (depending on the wind direction) and strung a double length of wire around the whole pen.

"That wire was expensive, but it will prevent them from escaping," he said.

"Yes, but it's made the whole thing a lot less movable."

"Hmm, that is true."

"It doesn't matter for now. They finished the weeds in there ages ago, but I've been bringing them plenty from the field, as well as hay and a little grain from the house."

"Yes, you are working very hard, much harder than me. When I have finished the final version of my book, I will become more active again."

"I don't mind," I said, happy for his studies to keep him out of mischief. "That's the nature of agriculture, isn't it? Very seasonal, I mean, although we should think about weeding the bean field again soon."

On returning to the car Manolo appeared to see the state of the field for the first time and scratched his head.

"Hmm, it is bad."

"Yes."

"You should have told me."

"I didn't realise myself how bad it was until recently," I said. "I come so often that I don't really notice it much," I added for good measure.

"It needs ploughing and weeding, but with the next rains the weeds will grow again."

"I suppose they will."

"Perhaps we will just leave it," he said.

"What? Abandon it?"

"Yes, why not? We would have to weed it several more times before we pick the beans and the crop will not be great."

"Luisa will be disappointed."

"Ha, I was thinking something like that. Nobody comes to help us and then when there are beans they will take them. Even I get tired of that."

"How about if we weed, say, a quarter of the field and you plough over the rest?"

"Ken, that is a brilliant idea. There will be just enough beans for my mother and ourselves. Tomorrow we will do that."

The next day we did that, before he returned to his scholarly repose, keen, he claimed, to finish the definitive version of the book before he began his night-watchman duties at the olive cooperative. There he said he would have many hours to kill and plenty of time to stitch the books together.

"What changes have you made?" I felt obliged to ask him that evening as we sat by the fire. "Have you made it less radical?"

"Ha, no, more radical, if anything, but I have ceased to think about the opinion of others. I have written my book in my own way and that is all. Perhaps in the future people will be ready for it."

"You might be right," I concurred, more than happy to push future literary analyses past my departure date. "Do you ever smoke the marihuana you grow?" I asked, not idly.

"Yes, I often smoke a little after you have gone to bed. It helps me to sleep."

"Why wait for me to go to bed?"

"Well, I thought you might not approve and I find it more useful when I am alone."

"Useful?"

"To stimulate thought. I smoke and look into the fire and have some very interesting thoughts."

"Why don't we have a smoke now?"

"Would you like to?"

Two minutes later he was opening a large tin containing the weed, a pouch of rolling tobacco and several packets of cigarette papers. Five minutes later he was handing me a lit joint.

"It is not very strong, but don't smoke much if you are not used to it," he said, as eager to take the joint from my fingers as I was to release it.

"Pepe and I used to smoke together often, but he decided that it was causing him paranoia and stopped, although he now seems no less paranoid than before, ha, ha."

After another long drag, he settled back in his chair and closed his eyes, a beatific smile on his face.

"Does it make you feel spiritual or anything?" I asked when he had opened his eyes and remembered to pass the joint to me.

"Hmm, in a way, yes, but it depends on what direction my thoughts take."

"I've read quite a lot about spirituality and different religions over the years," I said, not wholly untruthfully.

"Me too." He reached for the joint that had gone out in my hand and lit it. "When I finished with the Catholic Church I read a lot about eastern religions, such as Buddhism, and found it all very interesting; very different but very interesting. Why don't you pour yourself a beer? You are hardly smoking and I don't like to get high alone, unless I am alone."

I conformed with alacrity and brought a litre bottle and a glass to the little round table that stood beside my chair.

"I once studied to be a priest, you know, in Madrid."

"Really?"

"Yes, I expect Pepe told you and you are wondering about that."

"Er, he mentioned it briefly."

"Ha, I told you he was a terrible gossip. Yes, I studied for almost four years, missing the countryside terribly, before I decided that it was not for me."

"Why was that?"

"Oh, because of what I saw in the back of the shop," he said, meaning, I guessed, behind the scenes.

"What did you see… in the back of the shop?"

"Hypocrisy and corruption, just like in the real world. I shared a flat with three other boys. One was determined to become a parish priest because he liked the idea of having power over people."

"The power of the confessional?"

"Yes, that and just being *somebody* in society, somebody who people would respect. That one at least appeared to have some faith, but another boy was completely cynical about the whole thing and just wanted a safe, easy job and to have no worries."

"And the third boy?"

"He left not long after I did. For some time after that I was in a bad way. My father hadn't wanted me to study and when I returned he made me feel like I had wasted all that time, which I suppose I had. For some years I drank too much and only worked when I had to, but I didn't like that kind of life much either. I met a woman called Reme and settled down a little, but it was only when I came here and began to build the house that I felt my life had some purpose."

"I see," I said, feeling pleased but also a little guilty that my ploy had made him speak so frankly. I had no desire to probe into his state exam fiasco or anything else for the time being, so I told him a little about my own life.

"Yes," he said when I had finished, "you have had your problems too. I think I will go to bed now. Do you want the rest of this?"

"No, thanks. I'll just sit and finish my beer."

18

From that night on at about nine o'clock every evening, Manolo standing to walk to the storeroom to fetch his tin would cause me to head automatically to the fridge to get a litre of beer, or vice versa, and I must say that this moderate stimulus – rarely more than a litre for me and a single joint for him – took our conversations onto a higher, or at least more stimulating, plane.

Apart from talking a lot about the future of the project, we also touched upon spiritual subjects and both of us coincided in our belief in an immanent, transcendental God of some kind, while rejecting organised religion as unsuitable for our own ends. We agreed that the family as a unit was, on the whole, a good thing, but that matrimony was not for everybody and that some people had a more individualistic furrow to plough, a sensible point of view for me to have at the time, given the dearth of female company and the improbability of any eligible women who happened to pass by El Refugio (highly unlikely in itself) staying in our dusty-floored, breezeblock den for more than half an hour.

He also told me his version of the State Exam Scandal Hunger Strike, confessing only to having nibbled a little something each evening to keep his strength up, rather than putting away huge sandwiches, cakes and whatever else was available as Pepe had claimed. The truth no doubt lies somewhere between their two versions of the story. Shortly after this event he started seeing his first real girlfriend, Reme, a second cousin, who lifted his spirits and stabilised him for five years, before dragging him down and depressing him for the next five.

"It was when she insisted on us buying a new flat together that I rebelled," he said one evening as the rain lashed the house and watered the crops and weeds. "I began to look for a plot of land, just to cultivate, and I found this one. It was quite cheap and after I had bought it I had the idea of building a house on it. She was against it at first, then she was for it, then she was against us living here, so I started to build it anyway and we grew apart."

"Was it a painful separation?" I asked, beer glass in hand.

"More for her than for me. Once I started, I threw myself body and soul into the work and while I was building I conceived the idea of the project. Then I had no more time for television or shopping or evenings out. I found myself."

"And Reme?"

"She took it badly. Like most people, she has no real interests or hobbies, so our relationship was the only significant thing in her life, apart from her family. She has a son and a daughter from her first, her only, marriage who are slaves to the consumer society, just like her. It is better that you do not mention her to my mother as our separation caused some friction in our wider family circle. She thought Reme was perfect for me, of course, ha, ha." He threw the stub of his joint into the fire and took a sip of water. "After that there was Monica, who I think I told you about, but she could not have adapted to this kind of life."

"Are you keen to meet someone else?"

"Oh, I suppose so, but I will not go searching for her," he said, which was just as well considering the stained and shabby clothes he invariably wore. "Destiny will decide this matter, just like everything else."

After discussing the pros and cons of trusting to fate for a while, the conversation returned to the subject of women.

"I believe that you have to give fate a little help from time to time," I said. "To tell the truth, one reason for me moving on sometime early next year will be the lack of opportunities here to meet women. I'm not desperate, but I'm no monk, either."

"Ha, no, neither of us are, but feel free to take the car and go out whenever you want," he said, becoming more alert. "When Pepe is in good spirits I know that he goes out on Saturday nights, so you could meet up with him and see if the women of Écija appeal to you."

"I might do that sometime."

"You also told me that Isabel and Jorge from Seville invited you to stay with them. You could cycle to Seville along the quieter roads and spend some time there."

Surprised that he had remembered, I glanced at the rain drenching the gravel outside and said that I might just do that when the weather improved, at the same time thinking that once the first hint of spring was in the air, if not before, I would be making tracks. The thought saddened me a little, but I knew that Manolo would miss me mainly on account of all the duties he would have to resume, as despite our increasing intimacy since stimulants had been introduced into our evening routine, he was still very much a loner at heart.

We were both contented enough, but I hoped that something or someone would come along soon to shake things up, which is precisely what Pepe did when he visited us a few evenings later.

"Good evening, gentlemen," he said as he crossed the threshold. "It is like Siberia out there."

"The thermometer on the terrace said eight degrees just now," I said.

"Exactly. Inhuman conditions for an Ecijano. I have an email for you, Benítez."

"For me?" he asked, placing his weed tin down beside his chair. "What about?"

"About the project, of course. None of your mistresses would send me an email addressed to you."

"Let me see," he said, reaching out his hand.

Manolo read the email carefully, his smile broadening as he did so, before handing it to me. It was from a young man called Enrique from Salamanca who said he would very much like to come to stay at El Refugio for a few days in order to see if the project were suitable for him and if he were suitable for the project. If Manolo were well-disposed towards such a visit, he said, would he be so kind as to reply to the email, after which he, Enrique, would telephone to ask for further details.

"It seems very formal," I said. "He could just have phoned you."

"Yes, but he seems like a serious-minded young man," said Manolo, "and I prefer that to another weed-smoking hippy like the last one."

"Speaking of weed, what is that I see beside your chair?" asked Pepe with a grin.

"One joint does no harm, but now I do not feel like smoking. We must reply to the email right away."

"That will be difficult, unless Ken possesses one of those up to date mobile phones."

"No, just an old English one," I said. "I need to buy a Spanish one, really."

"In that case, we shall have to wait until I return home… or until tomorrow if I am too tired."

"No, no, Pepe, we must reply tonight," said Manolo, springing up from the rocking chair to find a pen.

"I was joking. Is poor Ken's company so tiresome to you?"

"Not at all, but the project must progress and this fellow seems like the right sort of person." He scribbled a couple of sentences on the back of the email. "There, I would be grateful if you would write this to him."

"I will do that," said Pepe, folding the sheet and placing it in his shirt pocket. "Am I to be allowed to drink my beer?"

"Ha, of course," Manolo said, before fetching three glasses and pouring most of the beer into them. "Here's to another potential member of the project," he said, clinking his glass against ours before draining it.

Pepe stretched his visit out a whole half hour before the exorcising powers of a mostly silent Manolo made him empty his second glass of beer and take his leave.

"Don't forget that email," said my suddenly jovial housemate on opening the door.

"If I did, I would not be able to sleep. Goodbye for now."

After I had locked the gate for the night I returned to find another litre of beer on the low table between us.

"I shan't smoke tonight in case he rings," he said by way of explanation.

"I doubt that he will ring tonight."

"No, I suppose not. I hope that Pepe did not think me rude."

"Probably, but I guess he knows how keen you are to get the project started."

"Oh, the project has already started, mainly thanks to you, but one more member would give it more... more prestige."

"Yes, I suppose it would."

At a time of such heightened emotions – his, not mine – I didn't want to remind him of my firm intention of moving on in the not too distant future, but after my recent reading of a Spanish translation of A Handful of Dust by Evelyn Waugh, I wondered what tactics Manolo would employ to persuade me to stay on. I hardly expected to meet the same fate as that of the young nobleman in the novel who found himself sequestered in the Amazon jungle and condemned to read Dickens to his captor until either of them died, but it *would* be rather handy if someone new were to appear soon to take over my duties. I hoped that this Enrique chap proved to have what it took to live at El Refugio if, that is, he ever got here.

Manolo and his chunky phone were inseparable all the next day and when the mare, plodding along as ponderously as ever, carried me home from my goat milking and feeding duties on the land, I was relieved to hear that my potential successor had telephoned.

"He will arrive on Saturday afternoon, in his car," an animated Manolo told me before I had closed the gate. "He is a Biology graduate who finds himself out of work at the moment. He is very keen on permaculture and ecological farming in general and sounds like just the sort of person we need."

"Great. We ought to prepare a room for him."

"I have already moved the boxes from the end room and my mother will come to clean and prepare it tomorrow."

"Can we not do that?"

"Of course, but she is coming anyway and says that she will bring some fresh sheets."

"That's good," I said, conscious that the frequency of our own sheet changing left something to be desired.

"I hope nobody will come to disturb us that afternoon," he said.

At half past four on Saturday afternoon, as we were sitting in the sun across from the shaded terrace, the long-lost Lola and a sullen-looking Mohammed appeared.

"Hello boys! I am sorry I have not been for so long. Mohammed here has been giving me a little trouble. As he would not even *try* to do his homework, I told him that until he did we would not visit you again. Isn't that so, dear boy?" Mohammed ignored her and looked longingly towards the chickens. "This week he has finally seen reason and has made a little more effort, so I agreed to come in the hope that Ken would take a little look at his books."

"Of course I will. It's good to see you both," I said, sensing (I swear) antipathy personified seated to my left. On glancing at Manolo I saw a brow more furrowed than the bean field and deduced that Lola's presence was not a welcome one.

When she went to visit the bathroom, he asked Mohammed to go to search for eggs and once the lad had skipped away into the chicken enclosure he leaned towards me.

"We must get rid of her," he hissed.

"Why?"

"Because I do not want Enrique to meet her; not now, not as soon as he arrives."

"I see what you mean, but at least it shows that we get visitors."

"On the phone he seemed to be quite a shy, serious person and I do not want that nattering woman to bombard him with questions. Listen, could you please help the boy with his homework quickly while I think of a way to make her leave."

I had no objection to getting my didactic chores out of the way, so I called Mohammed and suggested that we dispense with them as quickly as possible.

"Yes Ken, then I can play with the animals," he said, before we adjourned to the terrace table onto which he poured out the contents of his rucksack.

While we checked the Maths problems that he had completed almost flawlessly, I had one ear on the conversation taking place in the sun, wondering how tactless Manolo's ejection of them was going to be. The fragment that I caught showed a hitherto undisclosed side to his character.

"Reme is coming here?" asked Lola, astonished. "After the way you treated the poor woman?"

"Yes, she wanted us to meet to discuss our… well, to discuss things between us and Ken has agreed to go to the land so that we can be alone for a while."

"What things? You are not telling me that you might return to that silly, traditionalist woman? She is not good for you, nor you for her."

"Well, we just have to talk, so would you mind leaving when they have finished with the homework? Perhaps you could come to lunch next weekend."

As a consequence of this devious manoeuvre, a sorely disappointed Mohammed and an intrigued Lola left, promising to return the following week.

"Uf, thank God she took it so well," said the cunning trickster. "I hope she does not meet Reme in the street any time soon."

Perceiving my attitude of disapproval – we didn't know this Enrique from Adam, after all, and Lola was supposed to be a friend – he ventured an explanation.

"When she comes next weekend, Enrique will have settled in and will have seen what the project is all about. *Then* it won't matter if he hears Lola jabbering on for a while, but to meet her upon his arrival, no, no, that would not do."

"Whatever you say," I said, half hoping that this Enrique would turn out to be drooling wretch or a homicidal maniac (retired).

"The house is clean, his room is ready and there is fresh stew for dinner. I hope he arrives soon."

19

At shortly after six o'clock and with the sun already setting behind the house, a telephone call announced the proximity of our guest. Manolo, wearing a comparatively clean shirt and trousers as I had suggested, bounded up the drive to go to greet him at the roadside while I fully opened the gates to admit the car. The fairly new hatchback arrived a few moments later and both men got out.

I greeted Enrique, a short-haired, slightly-built, bespectacled chap in his mid-twenties and asked him if his journey had been a smooth one.

"Yes, I covered the 620 kilometres in six and a half hours, as the tom-tom suggested I would, plus an hour for lunch near Mérida," he replied in a far clearer and more precise accent than the ones I was used to. He was dressed in very rugged, new-looking clothes and shoes and had brought a huge rucksack and a small suitcase.

"Come, Enrique, there is just sufficient light to show you around here. Tomorrow we will visit the land," said Manolo before whisking him away and leaving me to take in the bags.

I was inside the house putting wood on the fire when they returned some ten minutes later, Manolo maintaining an enthusiastic monologue which Enrique listened to politely.

"Yes, permaculture is essentially what we are trying to achieve here, isn't it, Ken?"

"Er, yes," I said, not really knowing what it was.

"Yes," he went on, "everything we do regarding the crops and the animals is interlinked and sustainable. We use no pesticides or herbicides, recycle waste food and... well, we try to integrate everything."

"Do you recycle everything?" asked the sombre newcomer.

"Yes, all the food."

"I mean the rubbish as well."

"Oh, er, well, there are no recycling bins near here, but I had planned to begin to separate the little rubbish that we accumulate, yes."

"Ever since my student days I have recycled everything that I have used," said Enrique. "It may seem almost symbolic in this wasteful world of ours, but one must set an example."

"Of course, tomorrow 100% recycling will begin at El Refugio, ha, ha. Would you like a drink? A beer or a coffee?" asked Manolo, his face set in an ingratiating smile the like of which I hadn't seen since my initial tour of the house.

"I never touch alcohol or other stimulants, but a glass of water would be most welcome. As I have been living in the family flat in Salamanca, I must admit that my knowledge of permaculture is a theoretical one, but I am very keen to begin to put my ideas into practice and I am not afraid of hard work," he said, gesticulating with the soft-looking hands which until then had remained impassively by his sides.

"Here we are very keen on new ideas, aren't we, Ken?"

"Yes," I said with enthusiasm.

"Ken joined the project some months ago and is in charge of the animals. He has introduced more variety into their diet and they are flourishing."

"Do you recycle the animal waste?" Enrique asked me.

"Well…"

"Yes," interrupted Manolo, "the pig shi-, excrement will be taken to the land to fertilize the winter crops."

"And then there is the high nitrogen content of the poultry and goats' excrement, of course," said Enrique, sounding for the first time like the clever dick that I thought he might prove to be.

"Yes, that too will be used. I will show you your room."

After Enrique had descended the spiral staircase at about the same speed as Eustacia did, his face had assumed an even more pensive expression than before he had crept up it.

"What do you think of the room?" I asked.

"It is adequate, but if I were to stay for a long period of time I would like to plaster and paint it."

"Of course," said Manolo. "The plastering of the house is something I intend to do this winter, as well as improving the upstairs bathroom," he said, which was news to me.

"I am happy to do my own room, but I must first learn how to plaster," Enrique said before extracting a large mobile phone, tapping it, and laughing for the first time, albeit briefly.

"Ha, I will show you in half an hour and the three of us will plaster and paint the whole house in no time," said Manolo. "Let us eat."

While we ate the stew, which Enrique claimed to enjoy despite being *virtually* a vegetarian, Manolo kept up a stream of almost Lola-esque prattle about the future of the project, even suggesting spots on the land where Enrique and I would eventually build our sustainable homes. Enrique looked at his watch.

"Do you mind if we watch the news?" he asked.

"Of course, it is good to keep up with events in the outside world, however lamentable, ha, ha," said Manolo before standing to switch on the dusty set.

After the depressing political (corruption) and economic (doom) news, there was a short feature about some sort of gay-rights rally which I was scarcely paying attention to.

"Ha, such a lot of queers (maricones is the word Manolo used) all together. Now they are getting married, there will be a gay pope next, ha, ha."

Enrique stood up slowly and clumped up the stairs.

"Uf, and now sport. Surely we can switch the damn thing off now." said Manolo, oblivious.

As I sat quietly listening to the shuffling sounds coming from above, I put two and two together and came up with what turned out to be a correct deduction.

"Enrique is taking a long time," said Manolo a few minutes later. "Perhaps he is unpacking his things. I hope my mother cleaned the cupboard."

"She did," I replied, waiting.

"Ken, could you come up here a moment," said Enrique from the top of the stairs.

I went up and followed him back into the room where his bags lay strapped up on the bed.

"I must leave now," he said.

"Oh?"

"I am gay, you see, and I cannot tolerate the ignorant homophobia that I wished to escape from. My neighbours in Salamanca are quite prejudiced and I hoped to leave all that behind by coming here."

"Oh Enrique, I think it was just a silly remark. Manolo isn't homophobic at all," I said, having just realised that he probably was, at least a bit.

"No, I would not feel comfortable spending another moment in this house. It is so disappointing," he said with tears in his eyes, then more stoically, "It is not too late to find a hotel in the town."

"Why don't we all talk about it before you make your mind up? I think it's just a silly misunderstanding. I mean, to be honest, I could have made a daft remark like that, but it doesn't mean anything," I felt obliged to say, although I had concluded even before dinner that Enrique's stay here was not likely to be a successful one.

"It was the way he said it, in such a derogatory tone."

"I'll help you with your bags then. I'm really sorry that this has happened."

Once downstairs, Enrique explained in a very dignified way the reason why he was leaving and Manolo's pleas and excuses were so pathetic that I have no wish to reproduce them here. After shaking Enrique's hand and waving him off from the track, I returned to our enlightened, forward-thinking home. Manolo was already puffing on a joint and looking into the fire.

"Oh, well," I said as a conversation starter.

"Damn it," he said before taking another long drag.

"Well, if it's any consolation, I don't think he would have fitted in very well."

"No, I had never anticipated a gay person coming here."

"I didn't mean that," I said sharply. "I meant that I don't think he would have adapted very well to what we do here." He nodded gloomily. "Anyway, the advert worked," I said in a more conciliatory tone, "so somebody else might ring soon."

"I will be more careful next time. I will speak about nothing but agriculture for the first week," he said, giggling as the effects of the joint kicked in. "I am not very politically correct, you see."

"Yes, I saw that."

"But what were the chances of a gay man coming?"

"About 10%, I think."

"So many?"

"I think so, but with people like you around, they probably keep it to themselves."

"Ha, you are a good influence on me, Ken."

"One tries."

The following day and with no marihuana to dull his senses, Manolo was remorseful about his behaviour and remained melancholic for several days. We agreed that even though Enrique might not have proven to be the perfect addition to the project, it would have been instructive to have had a new face around the place for a week or two.

On the first Monday in December, according to the diary that I still kept assiduously – or I wouldn't be putting you through all this – Manolo received a call from the olive cooperative requesting him to report for duty on the following Saturday at 10pm.

"They always ring me because they know I don't mind working weekends and holidays and also because at this time of year they fear more thefts and must have a watchman present around the clock. I am not looking forward to it very much, but I will bind my books and earn some money in order to buy materials for the water deposit and other projects which will no doubt arise. It is only for a month," he said in a commiserating tone.

"I'll survive," I said, more than happy to have him off the premises, or asleep, for a few weeks.

Although the nights were growing colder and getting up of a morning was becoming an increasingly chilly business, the days were still warm when the sun was out, which it usually was, and I was looking forward to having the run of the place most of the time for a few weeks. This year he was to work a mixture of shifts and of the three main holiday events, Christmas, New Year, and The Day of the Kings on January 6th, he would only be at home for the first of them. It was with suppressed contentment that I saw Manolo off to work on the evening of our lunch with Lola and Mohammed, before which he had begged me not to mention Enrique's visit.

When I had been making ready to cycle down to Écija a few days earlier, where I planned to buy a phone and some presents, as well as paying Pepe a visit, his attempts at censorship had not been so successful. As Pepe knew about Enrique's intention to visit, I refused to airbrush him out of history, but did promise to play down his anti-gay gaffe on the grounds that our friend would no doubt spread the word far and wide, being the terrible gossip that Manolo insisted he was.

After buying a cheap mobile phone, a gift for Manolo and some lightweight ones for my two children – a leather wallet for him and a rolled up print for her – I posted the presents and made my way to Pepe's part of town, before making my first call on the new phone. Pepe's precise directions led me to an old, tiny-looking bungalow which turned out to stretch back a long way from the quiet street and possess a charming patio, where I leant my bike against the tiled wall. After introducing me to his mother, a resilient-looking woman not unlike Eustacia though a few years older, she withdrew to make coffee and we sat down in his book-lined study.

"You must be a keen reader," I said.

"Yes, but even I cannot read all day long. There is no prospect of work until February and I do not enjoy the festive dates that are approaching. So much materialism and empty conversation."

Not having expected these tidings of doom and gloom, I found myself putting my employment adviser's hat on.

"But surely you could find work in an office or something," I said, pointing to the modern computer behind him.

"It is not so easy. The small companies here obtain their workers from within the family circle and as for council jobs, well, I told you about our experience of the state exams."

His black-clad mother brought in a tray of coffee and biscuits, expressed her astonishment that I had cycled so far, and withdrew.

"It's only about thirty kilometres altogether," I said to my host.

"Ha, yes, but long-distance cycling is a mystery to old people. If you said you had come on a mule from Seville, she would have been less surprised."

"Did your mother use to work?"

"When she was a young woman she worked in the country, but when my father's building concern became successful, she stayed home to look after us. This house will be mine as I bought my two brothers' shares in it some years ago. They had their own family homes by then. My father died ten years ago, very suddenly, and I still miss him."

"I see," I said, sensing that this could be the cause of his periodic depressions, something that Manolo later verified.

"I sometimes worked with him and learnt a lot about construction, which was useful to Benítez when he was building his bunker."

"I thought he built it all himself."

"Apart from the roof, which several of his friends helped him with, he did work mostly alone, but if I had not been around to instruct him, God knows what he would have produced. I doubt that it would still be standing. Has that fellow from Salamanca arrived yet?"

After extracting a solemn promise that he would keep it to himself, I told him the whole story.

"Ha, that is Benítez for you! Oh, what a good story, but a promise is a promise. Can I tell my mother?"

"Is she a gossip?"

"No, she is a tomb. Ah, I forgot to tell you," he said, still cheerful after my news, "I have enrolled for English classes at the Adults' College in the new year."

"That's great."

"Yes, there are so many authors who I would like to read in their own language; Conrad, Whitman, Joyce, Faulkner and many more."

"Er, it will be a while before you understand writers like those, especially Joyce," said the veteran of three attempts at reading Ulysses.

"I know, I know, but one must have a goal. Perhaps one day you will write about your experience at El Refugio, as Benítez likes to call it."

"I doubt it," I said, which I did then.

"What are your plans for the future?"

I told him that much as I had enjoyed my stay so far, barring the animal cruelty and gay bashing incidents, and that I had learnt a lot about animals and a few things about horticulture, I really thought that I would have to move on soon, either to another savings-prolonging project or to find a job.

"Yes, to stay with Benítez for as long as you have is a great feat of endurance. Perhaps you will go to Seville or Cordoba and we will be able to stay in touch."

"I'd like that. Perhaps I'll look for an English teaching job sometime soon."

"Come to use my computer whenever you wish."

"Thanks, and perhaps we could go out for a drink one Saturday night."

"Yes, we could, but when the holiday season is over and I am feeling more animated."

After taking my leave of his mother and insisting that I had ingested enough calories to make the ten mile trip, I crossed the bridge over the river and climbed the long drag out of town, my stiff legs reminding me that another advantage of my month-long autonomy was that I would be able to go cycling more often. On several occasions when I had announced my intention of going out for a ride, Manolo had suddenly decided to plant some seedlings or bake some bread in the oven and I had felt obliged to stay to help him. Now I could use my month of freedom to regain my fitness ready for taking to the roads once more.

20

The fortnight up until Christmas was a very enjoyable time for me. The sun shone almost every day and by planning the bulk of my work around Manolo's waking hours at home, I managed to stay out of his way most of the time. His being offered and accepting extra shifts during this period meant that I felt very much in charge of the place and I began to wish that it belonged to me. Had it been mine, I would have planted olive trees on the land, kept the goats in the paddock at the house, and used the several strips of land within the walls to plant more than enough vegetables for my own consumption. With house and land prices still at rock bottom I began to seriously think about re-entering the labour market and saving up to buy my own plot, ideally with a little house already on it.

All this sounds like I had come to dislike Manolo, which wasn't the case, but after living cheek by jowl for three months it was a great relief to reassert my independence and the time that we did spend together was more enjoyable as a result. On several occasions he expressed his gratitude to me for doing practically all the work around the house and on the land.

"Last year I had a very hard time, rushing to get things done before going to the cooperative," he said one evening.

"Oh, it's my pleasure. I enjoy everything I do, apart from the weeding, and even that can be quite relaxing now that I'm used to it. I'm living here free too, so I'm more than happy to work."

"All agricultural work is therapeutic, I think, if carried out in the right way. My book stitching is also quite relaxing and helps to kill the time."

"How many books have you finished?"

"Three. It is very time-consuming, cutting the pages, stitching each segment and glueing them to the cover, but it is a labour of love. One copy will be for you, of course, but it shall be one of the later ones which should be neater than my first efforts, ha, ha."

During this fortnight Lola and Mohammed visited me on three occasions and Pepe twice, always when Manolo was at work. Mohammed was proving to be a passable student and an hour was usually sufficient to run through his homework, after which he would rush off to see the animals. I led him down the track on Yegua a couple of times and he soon showed signs of being a better horseman than me, though the mare's continued lassitude was becoming a cause for concern. On their third visit Lola asked me what my plans were for the holidays.

"Manolo is here at Christmas and I don't know what I'll do on the other two fiestas."

"Why not invite Pepe on New Year's Eve?"

"I could do."

"And as for The Day of the Kings, just make sure that you are here at midday."

"Oh? What's happening?"

"Nothing. Just be here."

On Pepe's next visit he said that the idea of coming here to drink a few litres of beer was his idea of a perfect New Year's Eve.

"A little drinking, a little chatting, and none of the stupidity which will be going on in town. You can count on me."

"Good, I didn't fancy spending it alone. For Christmas day I think I'll buy a turkey, or at least a chicken, and some other things for my lunch with Manolo."

"Do you seriously think that Doña Eustacia will allow you to cook for yourself at Christmas?"

"Well, no, but I don't fancy stew, again."

"Ha, there is no chance of that. Here in Spain it is Christmas Eve which is celebrated and you can be certain that you will not be without suitable provisions. I shall have to endure the nonsensical conversation of my sisters-in-law, but we all have our cross to bear."

On Christmas Eve Manolo got up at five in the afternoon after his nightshift and drove his mother back to town. On his return he opened the fridge and laughed.

"Ha, she always does the same thing every year, and more this year because you are here," he said after inspecting the roast chicken, platters of cold meats, cakes and bottles of cava.

"There are two legs of lamb and some roast vegetables in the oven."

"Yes, she always cooks me one of those, but the chicken is a new idea."

"In England we eat turkey on Christmas Day, so that might have something to do with it. It's very good of her. I tried to give her some money and she looked quite offended."

"At Christmas we are still children to her. My sister, nephew and some more relatives will eat with them tonight."

"I hope me being here hasn't stopped you going," I said.

"No, you would have been welcome too, but I have spent the last four or five Christmas Eves here alone. I hate the commercial madness of this time of year when people spend the money they have worked hard for so foolishly. I prefer to forget it all and if I do think about Christmas, it is of the birth of Christ, which they say used to have some connection with the celebration," he concluded with a mirthless laugh.

"Don't people go to church at Christmas anymore?"

"Oh yes, many people still go to the Misa del Gallo at midnight tonight, most of them after stuffing themselves with food and drink. To think that had I become a priest, I would have been performing such masses to people who attend once a year and have no belief." He shook his head and picked up his pipe.

"That sounds familiar."

"Ah, my mother left two parcels in my room for you, with a note saying that I am to give them to you tomorrow. Why is that, do you think?"

"Hmm, tomorrow is the day for sharing presents in England. They must be from my children," I said. (As Manolo refused to pay for a post office box, the little mail he received went to his parents' flat.)

"Yes, they seem to have come from abroad. Perhaps my mother has been doing a little research, ha, ha. Do you want them now?"

"No thanks, I'll stick to the tradition."

"Vale. Here we do nothing special on Christmas Day. The Day of the Kings is when presents are given, but I do not observe that practice. Tomorrow will be dull for you," he said, looking concerned.

"Well, a new country, new traditions," I said, wishing I had bought some sprouts.

"And I am working on New Year's Eve and the Day of the Kings."

I told him about Pepe's promise to see in the New Year with me and Lola's instructions for me to be in residence on the sixth.

"Uf, then anything could happen. She may bring a brass band. She seems to have been avoiding me lately."

"I think she suspected something about that Reme business when we were waiting for Enrique," I said, which although true enough, was not the reason for her avoiding him. She had told me quite plainly that she preferred to visit when I was alone, which I thought rather inauspicious for Manolo's dream of a thriving community built around himself.

The leg of lamb and vegetables were delicious, washed down with the beer, wine and bubbly which I had decided to indulge in liberally as I didn't plan to celebrate alone the following day. In the event, we did share a couple of litres of beer over our chicken and veg lunch, after I had telephoned my offspring and we had thanked each other for our respective gifts, a large Spanish dictionary from her and a leather wallet (great minds think alike) from him. I gave Manolo a new electric drill to replace the dangerously dilapidated one I had seen him using and he promised to sign my copy of El Sistema when he had cut, sewn, glued and bound it.

On New Year's Eve Pepe arrived at about nine and we put away several bottles of beer, laughed long and hard at some of Manolo's recent and more historical antics, before twenty minute's respite sobered him up enough to drive back into town, despite my offer of a clean-sheeted bed for the night. (If I seem to be whizzing through these important dates, it is because the events really weren't of any special interest, not because I'm as anti-festivity as my compadre.)

It was the next day, while Manolo slept, that I sat in the morning sun and had a good think about my future plans and resolutions. First of all I totted up my achievements so far and wasn't too disappointed with myself. Despite my advancing age, my Spanish had improved dramatically, albeit with a southern lisp that I found hard not to imitate, so I put that little feather in my figurative cap and turned my attention to my finances.

A quick calculation told me that if I had still been on the road, I would probably have spent at least €6000, as opposed to the couple of hundred that my stay at Manolo's had cost me. I'm not a materialistic man, but the thought of what I had saved sent a little shiver of pleasure through my body and erased the remnants of the slight hangover that I had woken up with. Had I not spent my time here, I reflected, I might have had to be thinking about ringing my boss Graham very soon and asking him if my mug was still in the staff kitchen cupboard, not an appealing thought at all.

On the other hand, had I not turned round on that drizzly September morning and ridden back to El Refugio, I might have been a kept man by now in the hacienda of some gorgeous, dark-eyed (and young) widow, or at the very least have found a steady job and got my residence papers in order, something I hadn't given so much as a thought to. Pushing these hypotheses aside, I contented myself with the not inconsiderable achievement of being practically as solvent as the day I had stepped off the plane, so after adding another small feather for my new animal husbandry skills, I turned my thoughts to the less than satisfactory aspects of my stay.

Apart from Manolo, I had made friends with his mother, Pepe, Lola and Mohammed, and while I loath to judge people by their usefulness, a utopian dreamer, an aged housewife, an under-achieving intellectual, an eccentric seamstress and a young refugee could hardly be said to form the core of a flourishing network of associates, not to mention the absence of eligible females within or anywhere near that group. This thought disheartened me momentarily until I had the happy, or at least consoling, thought that back in England and after three years of post-marital bachelorhood, I had enjoyed negligible success with the ladies despite knowing an awful lot of people.

All things considered, I concluded, I hadn't done so badly at all, but what of the future? Today was the day for resolutions (a.k.a. goals, if you remember) and as I hadn't succumbed to taking up smoking again, I decided that I had better come up with some fresh ones. Although I felt that my fiftieth birthday goal of *being somewhere I liked, doing something that I liked doing* would be achieved by that date – 26th February – whether I stayed or not, I now wanted to look further ahead and secure my future in Spain long before my money ran out. Another of my quick calculations, on paper this time, told me that if I stayed at El Refugio and spent no more liberally than I had done so far, I would be solvent right up to retirement age, upon which I could draw my pension and live out my life with Manolo, which turned my thoughts back to Waugh's man in the Amazon jungle. Would Manolo make me read his book, El Sistema, to him over and over again until one of us died? After laughing and shivering simultaneously, I brought my thoughts back to the present day.

The night before, Pepe had mentioned that the weather would now deteriorate and that night time temperatures could descend very close to freezing point. After enjoying many sunny days in December and conscious of Pepe's pessimism regarding weather conditions, and everything else, it was hard to imagine a sustained period of foul weather, but even a stoic Brit like myself had to admit that January and February were hardly the best months to resume my odyssey. Perhaps it would be best to see out my first half-century at El Refugio and set off shortly afterwards. In the meantime I could avail myself of Pepe's internet and do some research regarding my onward travels. Maybe in the meantime I would visit Isabel and Jorge in Seville, who Lola said were keen to see me, and visit a few language schools. Yes, two months would be ample time in which to plan my next move and break the news of my departure to Manolo.

On January 6th, The Day of the Kings, after hearing him set off to work one of the most unpopular dayshifts of the year, I got up and spent the cold, damp morning performing all my animal-feeding tasks, before showering, putting on some decent clothes, building up the fire and settling down to wait for whatever Lola had planned.

At shortly after twelve she and Mohammed arrived laden with bags, closely followed by another car containing Manolo's mother, father, sister and nephew. I hadn't seriously expected a brass band, but nor had I expected the mobilisation of Manolo's family by the indefatigable (and meddlesome?) Lola. His nephew Carlos was a handsome, strapping lad of eighteen and his sister Susana a pretty, petite brunette in her early forties whose slightly shrill voice was the only initial blemish I could detect in her. No sooner had they entered the house than Pepe arrived with yet another plastic bag.

"We would have come to eat the twelve grapes with you last night," said Eustacia, "but this old man goes to bed at nine o'clock."

"Always," said the old man with finality.

"What are the twelve grapes?" I asked.

"Did my miserable brother not tell you?" his sister chirped. "At the stroke of midnight one tries to eat twelve grapes before the chimes of the clock end."

"No, we were both asleep by then," I said.

"If you had spent the last twelve days alone with Manolo," chipped in Lola, already feeling left out of the conversation, "you would have been unaware of our traditions."

"Manolo is a strange boy," said Eustacia, shaking her head.

"Very strange," said his father, from whom we heard little more in the course of the afternoon.

"But all this eating and gift-giving has become too much these days," said Pepe, possibly trying to avert a bout of Manolo-bashing in favour of more eclectic conversational topics. "If Lola had not invited me today, my holiday season would have ended last night… but," he was tactful enough to add, "I am delighted to be here."

Between the three of them, Eustacia, Lola and Susana had brought enough food and drink for an Atlantic crossing (by rowing boat) and after a plethora of starters, we tucked into the roast beef and vegetables prepared in my honour, washed down by two bottles of red wine.

"Do you want a little glass, Mohammed?" said Lola.

"Drink is evil," he said gravely, before our guilty looks made him laugh. "Evil for me, but not for you Christians."

"I have yet to see you pray to your Allah," said Lola in a mocking tone.

"I pray in my room, and I am still waiting for you to take me to see the great mosque of Cordoba," he fired back sharply, indicating that Chez Lola was not the most harmonious place in the world and making me wonder if she regretted taking him in.

"I'd like to see it too," I said, "so when Manolo's car is free, we could both go."

"In that old thing? No, we will go in my car one day soon," Lola said, as I had hoped she would.

As young Carlos had yet to open his mouth, I asked him what he was doing at the moment.

"I am studying to be a car mechanic," he said.

"Is there plenty of work in Écija for mechanics?" I asked, unwilling to see him sink back into silence just yet.

"Not in Écija, but I will go where there is work; to Seville, or even to Madrid."

"Ah, you see, I bring you up and then you abandon me," said his mother with a wry smile.

"We should both go, to get away from my stupid father," he said, provoking a thoughtful silence around the table, caused, I thought, by his disclosure of family problems in front of a relative stranger.

"My ex-husband, you see," explained Susana, "cannot accept that our relationship is over. He pesters me and will not allow me to live my life as I wish. Perhaps we will move away when Carlos has completed his studies, but I have a job in a factory here and they are not so easy to find these days."

"Manolo thinks that you should build a house on your land," I said, fortuitously as it turned out, as the general laughter that followed swept the irksome family topic aside.

"My brother is crazy. One has to be where there is work as we do not all receive a pension like him."

"Two more years until I get mine," said Pepe wistfully.

Feeling full after the roast beef, I was dismayed to see the freshly cleared table soon laden with a variety of sweets, predominant among them a large ring-shaped pastry called a Roscón de Reyes, containing, I was warned, a small figurine of the Christ child which would bring luck to whoever found it. We were all pleased to see it turn up in Susana's piece, and Carlos's observation that he hoped it would make his father drop dead was received as lightly as I *think* it was intended.

The ice-cold cava washed this light pastry down quite nicely, but the several bars of chewy nougat called turrón that we tackled next made me fear for my ancient fillings and I was relieved that it was finally pushed aside when the coffee appeared. I say the coffee 'appeared' because despite my (mild) protests, I was not allowed into the kitchen area at any time during the afternoon. For the next hour or two as we conversed on a variety of topics I realised that Susana was observing me rather more than was strictly necessary and I tried to return her glances as discreetly as I could. She seemed to be a very pleasant, light-hearted lady, despite her post-marital problems, who I decided that I would like to see more of. After half an hour of intense thought the best I could come up with was this.

"Susana, I think that your field will need ploughing and weeding soon."

"Yes, I suppose it will," she replied. "I hadn't really given it much thought."

"If your brother ploughs the main part, perhaps we could all meet up one Saturday and weed around the trees," I said, glancing from her to Carlos to Pepe, who looked quickly up at the ceiling.

"Yes, that is a good idea. We could do that, couldn't we, Carlos?"

"I don't mind," said her son.

"Mohammed will be happy to help too," said Lola on his behalf. "It will be good practice for him and while you are there I will prepare a nice lunch here."

Although this was not exactly what I had in mind, it was better than nothing and we agreed to meet up as soon as a decent Saturday was forecast. Manolo arrived home at this point and, after drinking a glass of cava, agreed to plough the field as soon as he had finished his annual stint of paid work and also help out with the weeding. On this happy note, the party broke up with goodwill wishes all round and a bone-crunching handshake from the taciturn father into which he might or might not have injected some sort of message, it was hard to say.

21

Manolo finished work at the cooperative a few days later and while it was good to see that his energy and enthusiasm appeared to have returned, it brought my tranquil sabbatical (within a sabbatical) to an abrupt end. He had managed to stitch and bind thirty-six copies of the first edition of his magnum opus and the one he presented to me was considerably straighter and less jagged than his initial efforts which looked like the handiwork of a drunken mediaeval monk. The cover, produced using a marker pen, left a lot to be desired, but, as he said, it was the *contents* that were important.

"What are you going to do with the rest of them?" I asked him as we sat huddled around the fire one cold and inclement morning.

"Nothing."

"Nothing?"

"Nothing at all, unless anybody expresses serious interest in my ideas, in which case I will give them a copy. The book's time will come, and in the meantime I now have enough money to start thinking about the first important projects of the year."

"What are they?" I asked, quaking in my slippers at the thought of doing anything more than trudging through the mud to care for the goats, quite a task in itself.

"The main project is the water deposit, of course, but that will have to wait until the worst of the weather is over." (Slow, silent exhalation from me.) "But we cannot leave it too long as we want to catch some of the spring rains and also have plenty of water in the stream to pump up to it."

"About March then?"

"At the latest. In the meantime I will buy about fifty fruit trees which we can plant on the sloping part of the field."

"Apart from where the goat pen is, you mean?"

"We can easily move that, and if it rains while we are planting the trees, all the better."

I listened to the rain beating against the windows and drew my chair closer to the fire. By this time I had four blankets on my bed and rising in the morning was becoming more and more onerous, for him as well as for me, because the fact that whoever got up first lit the fire meant that it was sometimes well after nine before one of us threw back the bedclothes and braved the cold. As his bedroom was behind the chimney it never acquired the unpleasant dampness that mine did and if matters didn't improve soon I would have to buy that most unecological and unmanly of items, a fan heater. I never imagined that I would suffer more from the cold in southern Spain than I had ever done in my life before. (If you are reading this with the central heating on, spare a thought for me last winter.)

Notwithstanding my reluctance to even think about prolonged outdoor work, I felt obliged to remind him of one more task that we had promised to do.

"We are going to plough and weed your sister's land too, remember."

"Oh, yes, I had forgotten. Whose idea was that?"

"Mine, I'm afraid."

"Hmm, last year we weren't getting on very well and she paid somebody else to carry out the work. We must do it, of course, with their help, but I wonder why you..." A mischievous glint appeared in his eyes. "Is it that you find my sister appealing?"

"Er, well, not unappealing, I suppose."

"Yes, so they say, but I don't think she is right for you," he said with a shake of the head.

"Do you, I mean, would you not approve?"

"Oh, yes, compared to her ex-husband you are a saint and a scholar." ('Un santo y un sabio,' were his words, for the scholars among you.)

"Was he that bad?"

"Yes, she made a foolish choice when she was very young and in our society one still pays dearly for such errors. Free love is the way forward, ha, ha."

"That wasn't my intention; in fact I have no intention as such. I just like her and I suppose that's why I mentioned the weeding. Why is she not right for me?" I couldn't help asking.

"Because there is an insuperable intellectual divide between you."

"I'm hardly a cultural giant, you know."

"Yes, but you read and she does not. You can speak about many subjects and she cannot. It would not work."

"I think you underestimate her. Anyway, I'll drive out to the land to milk the goat now," I said, keen get off a topic that I hadn't even wished to get onto. I had taken a liking to Susana, but no more than that.

"I will go, if you wish."

"No, it's my job."

But for how long would it be my job? I asked myself as I plodded through the mud to the goat pen. It troubled me that Manolo was counting on me to help him carry out his projects and I really had to tell him soon that I would be moving on in no more than two months' time. The splendid food that his mother had treated me to over Christmas was still a very recent memory and it seemed rude to speak of jumping ship so soon afterwards. It occurred to me that nobody knew about my fiftieth birthday in six weeks' time and that if I let the cat out of the bag I would be wined and dined once more, causing my departure to be postponed yet again. I concluded that it would be best to keep my birthday a secret and get down to Pepe's when I could to do some research. Perhaps I *would* end up in Seville or Cordoba and still be within striking distance of El Refugio, so all my new-found friendships would not be lost. It was a bedraggled but pensive man who drove back to the house that morning.

After a week of almost uninterrupted rain, the sight of the blue sky through my rickety window blind made me heave back my pile of blankets, pull on an old purple dressing gown that I had found in one of the cupboards and rush downstairs to light the fire. After a hurried breakfast, I dodged past the seven cats that had remained with us and led Yegua out of her stable in order to give her some exercise after being confined to stable and paddock for so long.

I thought she would be delighted to potter along the road to the land once more, but after a few hundred yards I realised that her head was drooping and her gait even more ponderous than usual. Despite my having brought her oats, hay and a few capazos of greens to the paddock during the past week, as soon as we reached the track she made for the nearest clump of weeds, nibbled listlessly, and then refused to proceed.

Not being a whip-brandishing brute, I dismounted and gave her a pep talk, before tugging her gently along the track towards the steep slope which it took us several minutes to ascend. After completing my milking and weed-gathering duties, the return trip proved to be just as arduous for her as the outward leg, despite walking her all the way home. After leading her down to the paddock and giving her an extra ration of oats, I went to tell Manolo the worrying news.

"Hmm, she may be a little stiff after a week of inactivity," he said, needle in hand.

"I've never seen her like that before. Perhaps we should call the vet."

"Uf! The vet would charge a fortune for coming up here."

"I'll pay."

"Nonsense. Look, I see you are concerned, so if she does not improve in the next week we can go to see him and describe the symptoms. There may be some powders that we could give her. I have just twelve more books to sew together to complete my first edition of fifty, ha, ha," he said, pointing to the folded pages at his feet.

Feeling irritated by his lack of concern, I changed into my cycling gear and rode to Pepe's to do some research on his computer. After greeting my friend, who was busy reading Proust, I typed in some appropriate search words and after half an hour's reading concluded that Yegua had some sort of stomach trouble. It might be colic, in which case her dung would be harder than usual, or it might be bacteria, parasites, or even an ulcer. I learnt that horses cannot vomit, that stomach trouble could be very serious indeed and that horses were rarely operated on for digestive ailments. Not feeling inclined to perform more than a cursory search for a cure for my own malaise, itchy feet, I bade my friend adiós and cycled home, determined to monitor my steed's behaviour, and dung, over the next few days.

Two mornings later I arose to find Manolo absent and I was just settling down for a relaxing read in the warmish sun when he returned with a forest of twigs in the car.

"Cherry, plum, apple, pear and peach trees; fifty altogether," he announced cheerfully as he walked over to the terrace.

"What time did you go?"

"At eight o'clock."

"I would have liked to come."

"Oh, I didn't want to disturb you. This morning I woke up and said, 'Today is the day to buy the trees,' ha, ha."

"We could have called at the vet's too."

"Oh, I'm sure the mare will improve in this sunshine. Well, these trees are all of raíz desnuda (bare root) which one can plant in winter. They are much cheaper, but we should plant them right away. The car is very full so will you go to the land on the mare?"

"I doubt I'd make it," I said, glowering over my book.

"Oh, of course, I forgot. On your bicycle then?"

"I think I'll just stay here."

"Vale, yes, of course, I see that you are busy," he said with a worried look. "I will see you at lunchtime then."

After chucking an azada and a bucket into the car, he drove out through the open gates which I rose to close before returning to my book. When I had finished my chapter of One Hundred Years of Solitude, the first Spanish (Columbian, in fact) novel I had attempted and which I was finding quite challenging at the best of times, I relented and decided to cycle out to the land, reasoning that my annoyance with him would not lessen by staying put and brooding on his selfish ways. I would be leaving soon, I told myself as I pushed my bike past the mini-bean field, so I might as well help him with what might well be one of our last major tasks together.

Apart from a short break for lunch we spent the whole day planting trees on the slope around the goat pen which he had forgotten we were going to move, after which we gave them what seemed like an unnecessary initial watering.

"Soon I will install irrigation tubes to water all of them using the motor, until our water deposit is ready for use," he said that evening after we had showered, eaten and settled down in our respective armchairs.

"I think it will be time for me to move on soon, you know," I said.

"What? Oh, right. I hope it is not because I annoyed you this morning. I can be a little impetuous at times."

"No, of course not," I said, though his insensitivity to the mare's sickness had caused my resolve to break the news to strengthen throughout the afternoon. "It's just that I think it's time that I started looking around for a place where I can get a job and settle down."

"Vale," he said, reaching for the weed tin. (Pipe, weed tin, he always reached for something when he got the jitters.)

"Hopefully it will be somewhere not too far away, like Seville or Cordoba or a smaller town, so that I would be able to visit."

"That would be nice," he said without lifting his eyes from the evolving joint.

"And spend some weekends, and stay during the holidays," I said, suddenly eager to please.

On completing the joint, he placed it on the table beside him, stoked the fire, and turned to me.

"You can leave any time you like, of course, but it is a shame to miss the best time of year in the country. The spring is wonderful here and as the weather improves it is a joy to watch the crops grow."

"As I say, I probably won't go far."

"More people will come to visit at the weekends and I hope that we will get more response to our advertisement. Spring is the time when people will want to come."

'Throwing rope ladders over the gates,' I thought. "Yes, I suppose they might," I said.

"And then, of course, now that my sister feels more well-disposed towards me, she is likely to visit more often too," he said, playing what he thought might be his trump card with a poor attempt at a poker face.

"I didn't know you weren't getting on."

"About a year ago I told her some home truths about her life that she did not like. Since then she has hardly set foot in the place."

"What did you say?" I couldn't help but ask.

"I told her that she lived in a vicious circle of consumerism and that she ought to lead a more natural life and spend more time in the country. Perhaps she will like the country more now that you are here, ha, ha. Now I shall have a little smoke."

"I still think I need to move on and explore other options," I said as I rose mechanically to fetch my beer. "If I don't earn some money I'll end up back in England and one day I'd quite like to buy some land of my own, in Spain I mean."

"I believe that the field beyond my sister's olive trees is for sale and he cannot be asking a high price in such bad economic times."

"Well, you've said it. All the more reason to earn a few thousand euros," I said, unscrewing the bottle top.

"Perhaps you could teach English at a language academy in Écija. Then you could still live here and not have to pay rent as you would elsewhere."

"I looked into that the other day. There's only one proper academy and they require a special qualification which I don't have," I said half truthfully. There was only one half-decent language school, but I had no idea what qualifications they required.

Manolo took a long drag on his joint and looked into the fire so intensely that I expected to see steam emerging from his ears.

"What you need, I think, is a break," he finally said. "Why not go off for a fortnight, or even a month, on your bicycle?"

"Well, I suppose that's what I would be doing, really," I said, keen to get off the subject before he offered me dividends in his pigs or a timeshare on his land.

"That's settled then. When the weather improves, off you go on a little holiday and I am sure you will feel refreshed when you return."

Reasoning that as I had arrived with all my essential possessions on my bike I could just as easily set off with them, I agreed and we both settled down to enjoy our mild narcotics.

"How is the mare?" he asked some time later.

"About the same."

"We will go to the vet's soon."

22

With the air cleared between us, a prolonged spell of clearer air above us, and a marked improvement in Yegua's health, the month of January drew to a congenial close and I was looking forward to spending the following Saturday morning on Susana's land. I had finally telephoned my boss, Graham, who after spending five minutes urging me not to throw away my glittering career and five more congratulating me on being brave enough to escape from such a mundane life, became my ex-boss.

Burning my bridges, or one fairly robust bridge at least, had a mixed effect on my mental wellbeing. One minute I would be as happy as the proverbial lark, rejoicing in the thought of never returning to my depressing desk and 'customers' ever again, while the next I would be seized by a fear of the unknown which made me all the more determined to say goodbye to El Refugio and find myself a remunerative project of my own.

Still, as there was another month of potentially bad weather ahead of me, I turned my attention to the present and it was a cheerful Sr. Fretwell who greeted Susana, Carlos, Lola and Mohammed on a fine but still chilly Saturday morning. Manolo had gone ahead to the land to start the ploughing that he had judiciously put off so as to avoid weeding duties, so with him on his tractor and Lola in the kitchen, the two main obstacles to a free and easy conversation with Susana had been removed.

After placing the four operative azadas that I had managed to find in the boot, we drove to the land in Susana's small car and parked on the track between Manolo's land and hers.

"My brother's land looks very bare," she said, "apart from that little patch of beans."

"Oh, we've just planted lots of little fruit trees down the slope and there are more crops near the stream."

"Why doesn't he plant olive trees like everybody else?" asked Mohammed from the back seat.

"Because he is not like everybody else," said Carlos, still sounding sleepy after his early rise. "He has more modern ideas, I think."

"Shall we take a row of trees each and work our way down towards the stream?" asked Susana as she headed for the far side of the field.

I nipped in front of Mohammed in order to secure the row next to hers and after she had given us a very competent demonstration by hacking up the weeds around the first slim trunk, we each began our respective row. After warning an enthusiastic Mohammed not to chop down the tree itself, I began work on my own patch, at the same time observing Susana's rapid progress and, it must be said, her lissom figure encased in tight blue jeans and a pink sweat top. She might be a 'townie', as her brother claimed, but she certainly looked like no couch potato that I had ever seen. By the fourth tree I had drawn level with her and as Mohammed was still assaulting the ground around his third, I began to make conversation.

"You look like you know what you are doing," I said as she flipped a large weed aside and moved onto the next tree.

"When I was young I spent a lot of time up here, helping out in the summer. All this land was my parents' then."

"Are you not keen on the countryside any more?"

"Oh, I like it well enough, but I never seem to have much time to get up here."

"Your brother thinks that you should build a house and live here," I ventured.

"Ha, that is not going to happen. My life is in the town, where I can enjoy other people's company. I am not like him at all. Let us move on before Mohammed catches up with us," she said with a smile.

Encouraged by her apparent desire for privacy, I decided to test her reaction to my approaching departure.

"I might be back in a town myself soon. I'll be moving on in about a month as I have to get some kind of job if I don't want to end up back in England."

"Oh," she said, hiding any surprise or disappointment she might have felt very well. "Where are you thinking of going?"

"I don't know. I'll set off on my bike and just see where the road takes me."

"That sounds good," she replied, still hacking away.

"I might head up north to see what that part of Spain is like."

"Oh, it is beautiful up there. So green and much cooler in summer."

"Yes, I may head north, but I'll probably have a look at Seville or Cordoba first."

"Both are very pretty cities, but both are expensive to live in," she said, looking back at the progress of Mohammed and her son who were now neck and neck after the latter's leisurely start. "I prefer the smaller towns such as Carmona, Marchena and Osuna and it is possible that Carlos and I may move to one of those soon, if I can find work."

"Vale," I said, not wishing to pry into the reasons behind this, despite having a pretty good idea. "I might well take a look at those towns too. My best option for work is to teach English, so I may just ride from town to town until I find an academy that will take me on."

"I am sure one of them will have work for you," she said in a tone that made me think that it *might* have been meant as a compliment. "What does my brother think about you leaving?"

"He wants me to stay on, but I've explained that I need to earn some money."

"Of course," she said with approval. "Not everybody can live on a pittance like him. Hardly anybody, in fact."

By this time we were nearing the stream and about to complete our first row. I was getting attuned to her rather high-pitched voice and no longer found it irritating, but the faint rumble of Manolo's approaching tractor threatened to thwart any further confidences.

"I have a goal, you see. By the time I am fifty I want to be somewhere I like, doing something I like doing. I will achieve that all right, but I have to look ahead," I said, for some reason wishing her to know my age, but realising immediately that I had said too much.

"Oh, when is your birthday?"

"Er, quite soon." I looked over my shoulder to see Mohammed busy yanking out a monster weed.

"What day?"

"The 26th of February, but please don't tell anyone, especially not Lola. If they throw a big party I'll feel bad about leaving," I almost whispered.

"Your secret is safe with me," she said with a giggle. "Look, here comes the tractorista."

"Ha, you are making good progress," Manolo said after shuddering to a halt and switching off the engine. He had been ploughing furrows parallel to the stream and told us that once he had finished them he would then begin to go up and down the field. "That way it will be well-ploughed, although I doubt that you will finish around the trees before lunch."

"We can come back this afternoon," said Susana.

"There's no need. I will finish the rest next week," I said gallantly. By the time Manolo had moved on, Mohammed and Carlos had caught up with us, so for the rest of the morning I shared my sparkling conversational with all my companions, hoping to resume my tête-à-tête with Susana later in the day. By the time we headed back to the car we had covered about half the field and I realised that my promise to finish weeding the rest of it would keep me busy for a few days.

The heady aroma of fried chicken hit us as we entered the house, closely followed by Lola's strident greeting.

"Ha, the workers have returned from the fields at last. When you have washed, lunch will be served. Wash your hands properly, Mohammed, and your face too. Have you finished the work?" she asked me.

"Not quite, but I'll have it done by next week," I said, wishing that I had suggested another weekend work party, but loath to retract my promise now.

Twenty minutes later we were all seated around the table tucking into a large selection of tapas, including my old favourites, congealed blood and tripe, and slaking our thirst with ice-cold beer or cola.

"You have Susana to thank for most of this," said Lola from the head of the table, "as I only bought the drinks."

"Thank you, Susana, and thank you, Lola, for preparing this feast," I said.

"Oh, it has been a pleasure. We should do this kind of thing every weekend," Lola said, looking at Manolo, who kept his head down and his eyes fixed on the chicken wing he was demolishing. "Or every fortnight, at least," she added hopefully.

"It is Ken's birthday soon," said Mohammed, whose hearing and mischievousness were more developed than I had thought. "He will be fifty."

"Really? Your fiftieth birthday! When is it?" asked our self-appointed hostess for the day.

"Yes, when?" added Manolo, sensing a positive side to this revelation.

"Er," I began, trying to buy time, but soon realising that to push the date back would make me look silly in Susana's eyes and might make moving on even more difficult. I mean, even if I said July, Lola would begin to hand out the invites right away. (I thought all this in a couple of seconds, being pretty quick when my back's against the wall, but to no avail.) "At the end of the month," I finally said, glaring at the snitch.

"Splendid. That will give us time to invite Isabel, Jorge and anybody else you would like to come," said Lola.

"I don't normally celebrate my birthdays," I said weakly.

"Oh, Ken, but your fiftieth is different," she gushed.

"Yes, we will have to do something special," said Manolo, with his feet now firmly upon the birthday bandwagon. "It will also be a celebration of the end of winter," he said to me, "and of the beginning of the best part of the year in the country."

During these joyful declarations, Mohammed, on seeing my muted reaction to his treachery, sat looking rather shamefacedly at his plate, while Carlos remained as impassive as ever. His mother, on the other hand, observed me with a sympathetic smile which inspired me to make my boldest statement since asking my boss Graham for my life-changing sabbatical.

"Yes, my birthday, the end of winter, the start of spring, and also a kind of goodbye party as I will be moving on soon afterwards," I said, glancing at everybody in turn.

"Oh, where are you going?" asked Lola.

"I think I will explore the towns between Sevilla and Cordoba first, to see if I can find a job teaching English," I said, having realised by then that it was probably the most sensible move I could make.

"Ah, so we will be able to stay in contact," she said with a smile suggesting that she was quiet happy to have me installed elsewhere, as long as it was within lunching distance.

Manolo had lit his pipe by this time and over coffee he sat placidly puffing away while Lola made endless suggestions regarding the menu and the guest list, all of which I concurred with after first scanning his countenance for signs of opprobrium or distress. It wasn't until I accompanied them to the cars that I managed to have a private word with Susana.

"It's a shame that she spent all afternoon going on about the birthday party," I said when Lola had finally shut her door and turned her tireless tongue on Mohammed, who despite being a snitch must also have had some saintliness about him to put up with her day in and day out. "I'll finish weeding the field during the next few days."

"That's very kind of you. I will pay you of course."

"Don't be silly. It will be a pleasure."

"Perhaps next weekend we will come to visit so that I can thank you for your help," she said with a lovely smile. "I hope she will not be here, though," she added as we both waved them off. "I find her very tiring."

"Me too, and I think your brother feels the same."

"Yes, he says that he wants many people to come to live here, but he is a solitary person really, and not easy to get on with."

"I get on with him fairly well, but there's no future for me here."

"No, you were right to tell them that you were leaving soon. I could see that you found it difficult to say."

"Really?"

"We women are very perceptive. Until next weekend, then."

"I look forward to it."

The weather stayed fair for the next week and by extending my trips to the land by two or three hours each day I managed to finish the weeding by Friday afternoon. I had walked Yegua there on Monday and Tuesday, but on Wednesday I decided to ride and found her only a little slower than before her mysterious illness. On Friday Manolo said that horses had their ups and downs just like us, but I insisted that we must visit the vet if she relapsed.

"Of course, we will go right away. My sister will be pleased that you have finished the weeding."

"Well, it was good exercise."

"I take it that you got on well with her the other day, until Lola made any further conversation impossible?"

"Well, yes, we chatted for a while."

"She is a fine girl, really, and I wish she would take more interest in the country. She does not realise that in this ailing society of ours, the only decent future will be on the land."

"She said that they might come up tomorrow."

"Good! I have always wanted to spend more time with my nephew and try to awaken an interest in agriculture. Perhaps I will take him to the land while you and Susana get to know each other better."

I laughed at his clumsy matchmaking scheme. "There's no need for that, but I do hope that Lola will give us a rest tomorrow."

"Yes, so do I." He thought for a while. "I will call her and tell her not to come."

"She won't like that, especially now that she's arranging this party that I don't even want. I think I'll call her and ask her to come on Sunday instead."

"Yes, then it will just be the four of us tomorrow," he said, smiling benignly.

"Anyway, I thought you said that you didn't think your sister was right for me."

"Did I? Perhaps I was wrong. Watching her hard at work last Saturday reminded me that she is a country girl at heart. There is still hope for her, ha, ha."

"In any case," I said more seriously, "although I quite like her, I'm still going to have to move on and look for a teaching job."

"Yes, of course, but all jobs are difficult to get at the moment. Aha!" he exclaimed, pretending that he had just had an idea. "Have you not thought about trying to get some private classes in town? I am sure there are many people who want to learn English and you could use the car whenever you needed to."

"It's an option, but I really want to get a job and put my papers in order. I think I'm supposed to have some kind of residence permit by now," I said, having considered and dismissed his idea a week or two earlier. Six months, I had decided, was long enough at El Refugio, especially for a man about to commence his second half century. Exchanging a dull Derbyshire town for an isolated outpost in Andalucía was not my idea of an adventurous life and I wanted to see more of Spain before I settled down.

"But do you think you will stay in this region in the end? There are some fine towns not so far from here. Osuna is especially attractive," he said.

"Yes, I'll try to find something not too far away. Who knows, when I've saved some money I may look for some land around here," I said, keen to end the conversation on a high note.

"My sister already has some land," he said, raising his eyebrows and smiling.

188

23

Having spoken to Lola and convinced her that Sunday was the better day for her visit, I shaved and showered on Saturday morning with a sense of anticipation that I couldn't quite comprehend. All I was going to do, after all, was spend a little time with a woman who I quite liked, in the company of her son and brother, hardly an event to get excited about.

"My sister just called," said Manolo as I descended the metal staircase that now seemed quite normal to me. "They are coming for lunch."

"Vale, should we prepare something?"

"That will not be necessary."

"Oh, I hope she's not bringing all the food."

"Something like that."

An hour later as I greeted Susana, Carlos and... Eustacia I saw the reason for his cryptic comment and it dawned on me that Manolo's mother had postponed her weekly visit in order to chaperone her daughter. Whether mother or daughter had proposed this idea, I didn't know, but I carried the familiar canvas bags into the house and prepared to make the best of it.

Fortunately it was one of those bright winter days which, though bitterly cold at half past eight, had by midday become warm enough to sit outside, which is what we did once Eustacia had requested us to leave her alone with her stews. Manolo soon found himself things to do around the plot, even collecting the eggs for the first time in weeks, while Carlos plugged himself into some kind of game on his computer tablet, leaving the two of us to our own devices. Conversation was a little stilted at first as we exchanged ideas regarding the weather and the state of the economy, but feeling that our time alone might be running out, I reminded myself that I was a mature, confident, straight-talking man who knew how to call an azada an azada.

"How about if we go out for a drink or a meal or something one day?" I managed to ask after a few false starts.

"What? Oh, well, yes, I wouldn't mind, but, I don't know. It certainly couldn't be in Écija."

"No, but in Puente Genil perhaps, or anywhere really," I said, her embarrassment making me unsure that my proposal had been such a good idea.

"We'll see," she said more cheerfully. "We will see each other here in any case and when you leave we must stay in touch."

"Yes, of course," I replied, feeling almost relieved when Carlos pulled out his earphones and asked if lunch would be long.

Were Spanish women really so different? Was Susana's ex-husband really making such a pest of himself? Well, I'd asked her out and been rebuffed only mildly so there and then I concluded that her idea was the best one after all.

"I'll go and see if your mother needs a hand," I said with a smile that I hoped her womanly intuition would understand as meaning, 'Very well, then.'

Rising to the slightly more festive occasion of this Saturday lunch, Eustacia surprised me by sliding a tray of roast vegetables from the oven, which we ate with some delicious lamb chops that she had fried up. The stews were strictly midweek fare, she explained when I complimented her on her cooking, unaware that we usually ate of them at the weekends too, neither of us being keen on spending more time in the kitchen than was strictly necessary.

In the absence of Lola we chatted about all kinds of things, including Carlos's studies, gossip from the town, and life in England, which Susana seemed eager to hear about. When I told her about how much it rained and the insular lives that most people led there, she said that she guessed that life was better in sunny Spain, despite the harsh economic climate.

"Yes," chipped in Manolo, "and when everybody has to live off the land again, it will be much easier here. Here you throw seeds on the ground when it rains and they grow. You can plant two or even three times a year and never be without food. In the north of Europe it will be much harder for people to feed themselves."

"And what makes you think that we will all have to live off the land again?" asked Susana in the teasing manner that she reserved mostly for her brother.

"Oh, nothing really, just chronic overpopulation, the imminent breakdown of the capitalist system, possible nuclear wars, drought, disease. Those who are left will have to fend for themselves," he said with the old fanatical glint in his eyes.

"Are you listening?" Susana asked her son. "You are the only one who is young enough to have to worry about your uncle's crazy predictions."

"He might be right, though," Carlos said gravely.

"Good!" said Manolo with a little clap. "I don't mean good that it will happen, but good that somebody realises that our current system cannot go on forever. Carlos, you must come here more often and I will teach you how to survive on the land without electricity, gas or petrol."

"Yes, I will, if Mum brings me in the car."

"Cycle here!" Manolo cried. "Ken has the right idea. He cycles everywhere, or goes on horseback."

"It's too far to cycle. Mum, do you mind if I keep a little pony in the flat?" he asked in the same deadpan voice.

"Of course not, dear. It can live in the spare bedroom."

"Oh, you are the same as everybody else," said Manolo with a dismissive wave, not too annoyed by the flippant turn the conversation had taken and our subsequent laughter. Although Eustacia didn't play much of a part in our chatter, I could see that she was observing proceedings very closely and I wondered what she thought about her daughter's sudden desire to visit her brother again. Nothing much, it appeared.

Her inscrutability having given me no clues, Eustacia surprised me on the following Thursday when we were sitting alone on the terrace after lunch.

"There are still seven cats, I see," she said.

"Yes, seven regulars, with the odd guest from time to time."

"And I see that the pigs are fattening nicely."

"Yes, they're doing well now."

"I wouldn't give much thought to Susana, if I were you," she then said. I kept my eyes fixed on a small tabby until I had decided how to respond.

"We're just friends," was the best reply that I could muster.

"I know, and you are the sort of friend I wish she had more of, but any other kind of... well, anything more is not a good idea at the moment," she said, her normally playful eyes looking straight into mine.

"Why is that?"

"Well, for one thing her situation with Mario, her ex-husband, is a very difficult one. He is an unpredictable man and when he drinks he can make a nuisance of himself. Twice now Susana has had to call the police."

"Did they not give him a..." I began, but 'restraining order' did not yet form part of my vocabulary. "Have they not forced him to stay away?"

"Ha, the local police are useless. They drove him away in the car and nothing more. But apart from him, it is still not a good idea for her to be seen with you. Écija is a very traditional town and the people are great gossips. If you and her... well, no matter."

"No, what were you going to say?" I asked, having grasped that Susana must have mentioned my suggestion of a more intimate outing.

"Ken, I will be frank. If she were seen with you, a foreign man who is just passing through, it would damage her chances of finding another husband."

Stifling a scoff out of respect for her age, I said that surely people were no longer so old-fashioned.

"In the rest of Spain, I don't know, but in our town they are."

"Vale."

"Perhaps when you move on to another place and find a job you could meet her there, if you still wanted to, of course."

"That's just about what we decided the other day," I said, glad to be assured that I was not completely ineligible.

"It is best."

"Yes, so don't worry about it, Eustacia," I said.

"Ha! It is a long time since I heard that ugly name of mine," she said with a laugh. "Manolo! Come and drive your old mother home."

In the fortnight leading up to my birthday we saw no more of Susana, but rather more of Lola than either of us would have liked, as she appeared to feel the need to call round every time a new guest was added to the party list. It seemed to be turning more into her own party than mine, judging by the number of people who she thought I simply must meet, but she did ask me if I could think of anybody I actually knew who I would like to come.

"Well, there's Pepe of course," I said one afternoon when Mohammed's science homework had just been perused. "Have you invited him?"

"Pepe? Oh, him. I don't have his number."

"Don't worry, I'll be going to see him soon. What about Luisa?"

"Is she your friend?"

"Well, not really, but she's Manolo's and it is his house. In fact we had better ask him if he wants to invite anybody."

"Hmm, I have invited his family, but there are at least fifteen people coming already."

"I would still mention it, if I were you."

"Very well. Now, I don't know if you know the tradition in Spain regarding birthday parties."

"What's that?"

"Well, the person whose birthday it is normally pays for the food and drink, *but*, as I have invited many people I don't expect you to pay for it all."

"Oh, I don't mind," I said, not wishing to enter into tiresome negotiations. "I've spent little enough money while I've been here. Just let me know what I owe you. I'll give you some money now, if you like."

"Well, if you could give me €100 now, it would be a great help. Now, do you want me to buy the very best cava, or even French champagne?"

"No, just normal cava will do. I don't want anything fancy."

"Vale. Should I buy fresh prawns, or will frozen ones do?"

"Well, I don't really like either very much, but the frozen ones I've eaten tasted good enough to me."

"Vale."

She sounded disappointed by my frugality, but I was getting almost as fed up as Manolo of her meddlesome ways and wished she had never found out about my birthday in the first place. I would have much preferred to have a quiet goodbye lunch with *my* friends, before loading my bike and heading off into the unknown.

And it would be the unknown into which I was heading, after all, because when I cycled down to see Pepe the next day, I decided against doing any further research into my onward destinations.

"I managed with my map and a little guidebook before," I told him as we sat chatting in his snug study. "So I think I should do the same again."

"Yes, but be careful who you speak to when you pass isolated petrol stations or you may end up at another project," he said, his serious expression changing into a wide smile.

"Ha, I doubt that there are many more Manolos out there. No, I shall visit some of the towns around here first and see if I can find a job. It feels odd not to have earned a penny, or a cent, for six months."

"Hmm, I know that feeling well. At least you have not spent much."

"No, this party will probably cost me more than I've spent since I've been here."

"Uf! That woman is a public nuisance. You should not have given her a free hand."

"Well, it's too late now and it doesn't matter. I take it you'll be coming?"

"Yes, but I shall arrive late and leave early. I don't like big parties and I don't like goodbyes."

"It will be more of an au revoir than an adiós, I hope."

"That depends on you, Ken."

24

The last thing I had wanted to happen in the days leading up to the party – set to take place on the Saturday after my birthday – and my subsequent departure was for Yegua to become ill again, but when she stopped by the roadside on our way back from the land and I had to lead her home, I was determined to take action. Manolo's car was gone, so I telephoned him and told him that we would have to visit the vet's.

"Vale. I am in town, so I will go now."

"She's the same as before. I'm sure it's her stomach. Tell him that."

"I will. Don't worry, I will see you soon."

On his return he produced two boxes, one containing some powders to mix into her oats, and the other some antibiotic capsules and a hypodermic syringe with which to inject the liquid into her neck.

"Which did he say to use first?" I asked after reading the rather puzzling notes.

"He said that if her shit looks normal, we should inject the antibiotics."

"It does, to me, but I don't fancy doing the injection."

"Don't worry, I have done it before, to a donkey of my father's."

"Did it work?"

"The donkey was very old. Come, you can hold her head while I inject."

Yegua only winced slightly at the stab of the needle and as the day was quite warm, I took her down to the paddock and gave her some oats and plenty of hay. That evening when I led her up the path she seemed no better, but on the following afternoon I was pleased to see her come walking briskly towards me from the far side of the paddock and I breathed a sigh of relief. It would have been very difficult to leave an ailing Yegua behind me and I had decided to set off on the day after the party.

It rained all day Friday, good news for the crops and the new trees, but making us fear that we would be spending the following day at very close quarters with Lola's invitees.

"When you have gone, I think I will find a way to break off relations with Lola," Manolo said during our last peaceful fireside chat. "She is becoming insupportable, as she has done in the past, and I need a rest from her."

"How will you manage that? To break off relations, I mean."

"Oh, I will think of a way to offend her. Nothing too nasty, but enough to keep her away for a while. As I may have to build the water deposit alone, I will need to rest in the evenings, not listen to the nonsense of somebody who is not in the least interested in the project."

As the water deposit had reared its guilt-inducing head, I sipped my beer for a while in order to avoid making any empty promises. Fortunately, Manolo had a little revelation lined up.

"*But*, I did receive a most welcome call this morning. A man from Valencia wishes to visit El Refugio next month."

"That's great news," I said. "What's he like?"

"Well, he seems to be the right sort of person. He is thirty-two and gave up his job as a security guard in order to go to Peru to live with the Indians there, high in the mountains. He spent several months with them and told me that the only meat they ate was rat, roast rat, so my mother's stews ought to be an improvement, ha, ha."

"Your mother's stews are delicious. What else did he say?"

"Oh, that he learnt how to grow crops at high altitude and how to speak a little of their language. The important thing is that he is interested in the project. He seemed very enthusiastic."

"Perhaps he'll look after the animals."

"Ha, I hope so." He picked up his freshly-rolled joint and put it down again. "Now, what I want to know is, do I give him your room, or do I install him in another room in case you return?"

"Well..." I began, torn between a diplomatic answer and a straight one. "My room is the best one upstairs, so give him that. If I return I can use the one at the end that Enrique almost slept in," I said, combining directness, diplomacy and a warning rather deftly, I thought.

"Yes, I will remember Enrique when this man, Vicente, arrives and I will be careful not to offend him, ha, ha."

"A young chap like that should be a big help with the water deposit," I said.

"Yes, that is what I hope." He lit the joint and snuggled down in his chair. "The nature of an undertaking of this type is that people will come and go. Eventually there will remain a nucleus of people who are committed to the project."

Either that or committed to an asylum, I thought, but just nodded. Now there was only this dratted party to get through and I would be on my way.

The day of Lola's party, which is how both Manolo and I thought of it, dawned bright and by nine o'clock I had ridden Yegua to the land to feed and say goodbye to the goats and milk the sole productive one for the last time. She was giving less milk by now and Manolo had told me that he was going to invest in a decent billy goat to get things moving again, as the two oldies had shown no inclination to mount the females, unless they did it when I wasn't around out of modesty. I urged him to take them back down near to the stream now that winter was practically over, as I knew he wouldn't make the same effort as I had to supply them with their daily ration of green edibles. I was less concerned about the pigs and poultry as feeding them was straightforward and they were much closer to home, but I feared for the future of Yegua and extracted a promise that he would take her out to pasture most days.

When I returned to the house Lola had already staked her claim to the kitchen area and, with Mohammed's help, was unloading a lot of trays and containers and placing them in the fridge or on the kitchen tops. When I realised how much time she must have spent preparing all the dishes I felt a little guilty about thinking ill of her and I thanked her profusely for her efforts.

"It is my pleasure, and there is more to come as Eustacia and Susana have also been hard at work. You and Manolo must monitor the freezer to make sure that all the bottles do not freeze. Put them on the garage floor or in the fridge when they are cold."

Eustacia, Susana and Carlos arrived soon after and when the ladies had left everything in position for the subsequent frying, heating or dishing out, we congregated on the terrace to await the guests.

I won't give you the life story of every one of the guests, but apart from Pepe, Isabel, Jorge, Luisa and her children Pablo and Paloma, all the others were unknown to me. There was Luisa's husband, Jose, a pleasant but anxious-looking chap; Rafael, a balding bar owner from Écija who was rumoured to be Lola's latest flame; a jolly middle-aged couple who were in the bakery trade; an ex-local councillor who looked like a drinker and was; and two more men and a woman who I was only introduced to briefly.

I decided that today wasn't the day for making new friends, but during the course of the meal, served as a buffet on the terrace and in the house, I made a point of spending a little time with everybody I knew in a roughly ascending order of significance to me. After a predictably inane exchange with Luisa, I sought out Isabel and Jorge and explained how bad weather and other factors had stopped me from visiting them, but that now I was a free agent again and would probably be heading in their direction, I would almost certainly pay them a visit during the next few weeks. After chatting for a while and exchanging phone numbers, I went to look for Pepe, who I found hiding round the side of the house with a glass of beer and a plate of fried cheese.

"There you are," I said.

"This is not my sort of gathering, Ken. I know the Ecijanos by sight but have no desire to speak to them. I will leave soon, but you must phone me when you have found a place to live and I will visit you."

"If it's not too far away."

"If it is in the south of Spain it will not be too far away. I will miss you."

"Me too. I have a feeling that I won't be leaving Andalucía. Why would I head north if I have friends here?"

"Exactly."

"Come, I will introduce you to a nice couple from Seville," I said, before taking him over to Isabel and Jorge, with whom he spent the rest of the afternoon chatting happily.

I didn't know if birthday cakes were the order of the day in Spain and I rather hoped they weren't, but when Lola disappeared after coffee had been served I feared the worst. Sure enough, just as we were helping ourselves to sugar, milk or brandy, Mohammed was thrust through the door with a candlelit cake in his hands, upon which Lola commenced a spirited rendition of 'Cumpleaños Feliz'. (Same tune, different words.) The other guests joined in with varying degrees of melody and enthusiasm, after which I was obliged to blow the candles out, something I managed by filling my lungs and exhaling very slowly, picking off the candles one by one.

"That is English ingenuity!" cried the ex-councillor, who had to be led to Manolo's room to rest shortly afterwards. Apart from that bloated burgher, however, there was none of the drunkenness and certainly none of the weed smoking that had occurred at the Green Party bash, and after I had received my presents, the ordeal was more or less over.

I thought the choice of presents interesting, considering that the next day I would be setting off on my bicycle with all my worldly possessions on board. Manolo had bought me nothing, which was easy enough to carry, while the (hideous) framed picture that I received from Luisa would prove to be a menace in high winds, if I'd had the slightest intention of taking it with me. Pepe gave me a handsome copy of Lorca's poetry, while Lola's offering of a huge rucksack will have to be stored well out of sight by Manolo until he passes it on to a new owner, perhaps someone fleeing from the project. Isabel and Jorge gave me a 'Los Verdes' t-shirt which I shall wear with pride, but the best gift of all was from Susana, a red, short-sleeved cycling top into whose back pocket she slipped her telephone number when I had unfolded it.

"Thanks, Susana. I'll wear it tomorrow if it's sunny, and I'll give you a call soon."

"I hope so. Take care on the roads."

"I will," I said, and she disappeared through the gate.

I gave Eustacia two kisses that she had not been expecting, thanked her for everything, and went to my room for a while until Lola had dispatched all *her* guests, after which I settled my account with her and promised to telephone sometime soon.

I spent most of the evening packing and the next morning, another sunny one, Manolo accompanied me up the drive to the gate.

"Well, you know where I am," he said as we shook hands.

"Yes, and I'm sure I'll be back. How soon, I don't know. Thanks for letting me stay for so long."

"Ha, no, thank *you* for helping me so much. Well, take a look at the world out there and come back whenever you wish."

"I will, and I'll call you in a week or so. I hope the next visitor, Vicente, turns out all right."

"Me too. Adiós, Ken."

"Hasta la vista," I said as I wheeled my bike up the track.

On reaching the road I got on the bike, decided whether to turn right or left, and set off.

Ken Fretwell,
Somewhere in Spain,
November 2014

Printed in Great Britain
by Amazon

30177728R00116